THE ROAD AHEAD
MIDDLE EAST POLICY IN THE BUSH ADMINISTRATION'S SECOND TERM

PLANNING PAPERS FROM THE
SABAN CENTER FOR MIDDLE EAST POLICY
AT THE BROOKINGS INSTITUTION

EDITED BY FLYNT LEVERETT
WITH CONTRIBUTIONS BY:
MARTIN INDYK
KENNETH POLLACK
JAMES STEINBERG
SHIBLEY TELHAMI
TAMARA COFMAN WITTES

Copyright © 2005
THE BROOKINGS INSTITUTION
1775 Massachusetts Avenue, N.W., Washington, D.C. 20036
www.brookings.edu

The Road Ahead:
Middle East Policy in the Bush Administration's Second Term
may be ordered from:
Brookings Institution Press
1775 Massachusetts Avenue, N.W.,
Washington, D.C. 20036
Tel. 1-800/275-1447 or 202/797-6258
Fax: 202/797-2960
www.bookstore.brookings.edu

Library of Congress Cataloging-in-Publication data are available
ISBN-13: 978-0-8157-5205-9
ISBN-10: 0-8157-5205-9

The paper used in this publication meets minimum requirements of the American National Standard for Information Sciences—Permanence of Paper for Printed Library Materials: ANSI Z39.48-1992.

9 8 7 6 5 4 3 2

TABLE OF CONTENTS

MARTIN INDYK

Martin Indyk is director of the Saban Center for Middle East Policy at the Brookings Institution. He has served as special assistant to the president and senior director for Near East and South Asia in the National Security Council and as assistant secretary of state for Near East Affairs. As a member of President Clinton's peace team, he also served twice as U.S. ambassador to Israel. He is currently completing a book on Clinton's diplomacy in the Middle East.

FLYNT LEVERETT

Flynt Leverett is a senior fellow at the Saban Center. He was senior director for Middle East affairs at the National Security Council, advising the White House on relations with Egypt, Israel, Jordan, Lebanon, the Palestinian Authority, Saudi Arabia, and Syria. He previously served as a Middle East and counterterrorism expert on the Secretary of State's Policy Planning Staff and as a senior CIA analyst. He is the author of the forthcoming book *Inheriting Syria: Bashar's Trial by Fire* (April 2005), and is currently at work on a book about the future of Saudi Arabia.

KENNETH POLLACK

Kenneth Pollack is director of research at the Saban Center. He previously served as a CIA analyst and as the National Security Council's director for Persian Gulf affairs and for Near East and South Asian affairs. His new book, *The Persian Puzzle: The Conflict between Iran and America* (November 2004), examines the troubled history of U.S.-Iranian relations and offers a new strategy for U.S. policy towards Iran. He is also the author of *The Threatening Storm: The Case for Invading Iraq* and *Arabs at War: Military Effectiveness, 1948–1991* (both 2002).

JAMES STEINBERG

James Steinberg is vice president and director of the Foreign Policy Studies Program at the Brookings Institution. Prior to joining Brookings he was a senior advisor at the Markle Foundation. Mr. Steinberg also held several senior positions in the Clinton Administration, including deputy national security advisor and director of the Policy Planning Staff at the U.S. Department of State. His previous positions include deputy assistant secretary for regional analysis in the Bureau of Intelligence and Research at the State Department and senior analyst at RAND. Mr. Steinberg is the author of and contributor to many books on foreign policy and national security topics, as well as domestic policy, including *Protecting the American Homeland* and *An Ever Closer Union: European Integration and Its Implications for the Future of U.S.-European Relations.*

Shibley Telhami

Shibley Telhami is a nonresident senior fellow at the Saban Center. He is the Anwar Sadat Professor at the University of Maryland and author of *The Stakes: America and the Middle East* (2002). His many other publications on Middle East politics include *Power and Leadership in International Bargaining: The Path to the Camp David Accords* (1990). His current research focuses on the media's role in shaping Middle Eastern political identity and the sources of ideas about U.S. policy in the region.

Tamara Cofman Wittes

Tamara Cofman Wittes is a senior fellow at the Saban Center. She previously served as Middle East specialist at the U.S. Institute of Peace and director of programs at the Middle East Institute. Her work has addressed a wide range of topics, including the Israeli-Palestinian peace negotiations, humanitarian intervention, and ethnic conflict. Her current research focuses on U.S. policy toward democratization in the Arab world and the challenge of regional economic and political reform. She is the author of the forthcoming book *How Israelis and Palestinians Negotiate: A Cross Cultural Analysis of the Oslo Peace Process* (2005).

INTRODUCTION:
BUSH AND THE MIDDLE EAST

Flynt Leverett

Confronting a terrorist threat that struck the American homeland on September 11, 2001, President George W. Bush responded by laying out a bold foreign policy and national security strategy with few precedents in the modern record of American diplomacy. To deal with the threat of global terror, Bush did not explore a reconfiguration of the global balance of power, as, in very different ways, his father had at the end of the Cold War and Richard Nixon had in the early 1970s. Bush did not propose the creation of a new network of alliances, as Harry Truman did at the outset of the Cold War. Likewise, Bush did not call for the development of new international institutions or a system of collective security, as Franklin Roosevelt had envisioned rising out of the rubble and ashes of World War II.

Rather, facing the defining challenge of his presidency, Bush developed and pursued a policy approach that can be described as Wilsonian (or, perhaps, Reaganesque) in its ambition to secure America by changing the political orientation of states in far-flung parts of the globe. As this ambitious agenda took shape, it became increasingly clear that President Bush's approach to securing American interests in the post-9/11 world was focused primarily on the Middle East, defined broadly to include important non-Arab states in the Muslim world, such as Afghanistan, Iran, and Turkey.

AN AMBITIOUS AGENDA

Speaking just nine days after the September 11 attacks, the president declared war not simply on Usama bin Ladin and the jihadists that had struck the United States, but on all terrorism "with global reach." In the process, Bush articulated a maximalist vision for victory in that struggle. The United States would not content itself with destroying terrorist cells and organizations around the world; those states that, in Washington's view, support terrorist activity would have to choose whether they stood with the civilized world or with the terrorists.

In the fall of 2001, the United States launched a military campaign to unseat the Taliban regime in Afghanistan that had given bin Ladin and his followers safe haven, as well as to root out the al-Qa'ida leadership from its sanctuaries there. But it was not clear, at the outset of Operation Enduring Freedom, whether the United States was acting primarily to eliminate a specific terrorist threat through a "decapitation" strategy against al-Qa'ida or to launch a sustained campaign to remake the Arab and Muslim worlds—in terms of both the strategic balance in the broader Middle East and prevailing models of governance across the region.

In the early stages of the war on terror, the fight against al-Qa'ida provided the impetus for a dramatic upturn in counterterrorism cooperation between the United States and governments around the world. The struggle against al-Qa'ida and related groups also prompted an unprecedented degree of official U.S. engagement with the problems of public diplomacy toward the Muslim world, with the aim of undercutting the appeal of Islamist extremism.

But President Bush's maximalist aspirations became increasingly apparent as the war progressed. In particular, the president broadened the focus of the war on terror to encompass an entire category of "rogue" regimes. In his January 2002 State of the Union address, Bush underscored his concern about those state sponsors of terrorism that were simultaneously pursuing weapons of mass destruction (WMD)—especially nuclear weapons—and oppressing their own peoples. Three such states—Iran, Iraq, and North Korea—were enshrined in the address as members of an "axis of evil." A prospective link between ties to terrorist groups and pursuit of WMD capabilities was subsequently adduced by the Administration to justify military intervention to unseat Saddam Hussein's regime in Baghdad—a regime that had no demonstrable involvement in the September 11 attacks and, as the U.S. Intelligence Community argued at the time and the 9/11 Commission concluded in retrospect, no meaningful operational ties to al-Qa'ida.

In the months that followed the 9/11 attacks, Bush also made clear that he was determined to address what he considered the root causes of the terrorist threat confronting the United States and its democratic allies—as the president sometimes put it, to "drain the swamp" in which terrorist recruits were bred. The president proposed to do this by nothing short of remaking the Arab and Muslim worlds. As the president's 2002 National Security Strategy operationalized this idea, the United States would strive to diminish "the underlying conditions that spawn terrorism by enlisting the international community to focus its efforts and resources on areas most at risk" and by "supporting moderate and modern government, especially in the Muslim world, to ensure that the conditions and ideologies that promote terrorism do not find fertile ground in any nation."

Bush's transformative agenda for what would come to be called the broader Middle East had at least two foundational aspects. First, with regard to regional conflicts, the president embraced a two-state solution to the Israeli-Palestinian conflict more fully than any of his predecessors. In contrast to President Clinton, who publicly endorsed the notion of Palestinian statehood only during his last month in office and as an "idea" that would be taken off the table at the end of his term, Bush made the establishment of a Palestinian state a high-profile element of his Administration's declaratory foreign policy, laying out his position in clear language before the United Nations General Assembly in November 2001. (Indeed, one of the president's undeniable achievements in the Arab-Israeli arena has been to normalize discussion of Palestinian statehood in the United States and in Israel.)

Second, Bush articulated a vision of democratic and market-oriented reform for the Arab and Muslim worlds, ascribing a higher priority to promoting positive internal change in Middle Eastern countries than any of his predecessors. To implement this vision, the president proposed a number of important policy initiatives, including a Middle East Trade Initiative aimed at the eventual creation of a Middle East Free Trade Area and a Greater Middle East Initiative for reform, which, in collaboration with the G-8, became the Broader Middle East and North Africa initiative.

The president also linked his quest for democratization in the Arab and Muslim worlds to his policy approaches for Iraq and the creation of a Palestinian state. Bush has repeatedly argued that the establishment of a democratic Iraq, "in the heart of the Middle East," would have a transformative effect across the region. Similarly, he has argued that the establishment of a democratically legitimated Palestinian leadership free from the taint of corruption and terror is essential to achieving a two-state solution to the Israeli-Palestinian conflict.

As the president embarked on his second term in office, he reaffirmed his commitment to this transformative agenda. In his second inaugural address, Bush noted that "as long as whole regions of the world simmer in resentment and tyranny—prone to ideologies that feed hatred and excuse murder—violence will gather, and multiply in destructive power, and cross the most defended borders, and raise a mortal threat." There is, Bush argued, "only one force in history that can break the reign of hatred and resentment, and expose the pretensions of tyrants, and reward the hopes of the decent and tolerant, and that is the force of human freedom." On the basis of this analysis, Bush declared, "It is the policy of the United States to seek and support the growth of democratic movements and institutions in every nation and culture, with the ultimate goal of ending tyranny in our world."

A Region in the Balance

From this review, it is clear that Bush's stewardship of the war on terror and his foreign policy more generally will be judged primarily by their efficacy and impact in the Middle East. It is also clear that, at this writing, the success or failure of the Administration's policies in that essential region hangs very much in the balance.

In the essays that follow, the fellows of the Brookings Institution's Saban Center for Middle East Policy (along with James Steinberg, vice-president and director of Foreign Policy Studies at Brookings) offer their recommendations as to how the Bush Administration might yet complete the ambitious agenda it has defined for itself in the broader Middle East. Some of the authors might not agree with all of the arguments advanced in pieces composed by their colleagues. Nevertheless, all of the essays start with some common analytic judgments about the Bush Administration's first-term foreign policy record and some common assumptions about how best to move forward.

One of the principal assessments animating all the essays is that the Bush Administration's handling of the core policy challenges in the Middle East has been suboptimal, at best. On multiple fronts—the fight against terror rooted in Islamist extremism, post-conflict stabilization and reconstruction in Iraq, and dealing with the threat posed by other regional rogues (such as Iran and Syria)—current trends are not positive; a straight-line continuation of the status quo on these issues could well prove disastrous for U.S. interests in the region.

The Administration's difficulties in prosecuting the global war on terror illustrate well this basic point. The "war on terror" may have been the single most important conceptual and rhetorical framework shaping President Bush's foreign policy during his first term, but, within a few months after the 9/11 attacks, this framework had begun to lose its focus as a framing device for policy.

In particular, the decision to prepare for and, ultimately, to launch Operation Iraqi Freedom was never accepted as an integral part of the war on terror by large parts of the international community. In the aftermath of the September 11 attacks, the United States had the support of virtually the entire international community for a military campaign to unseat the Taliban in Afghanistan and for other actions to eliminate the threat of further attacks by al-Qaʿida. By shifting its focus to Iraq, where the justification for urgent, forcible regime change was perceived in many quarters as less clear cut, the Bush Administration lost a significant measure of that support. And, as Iraq became ever more the centerpiece of the Administration's game plan for the war on terror, the effectiveness of its "decapitation" strategy against al-Qaʿida started to decline.

This created a "breathing space" within which the nature of the jihadist threat began to shift. Over the last three years, al-Qaʿida has become a relatively small component of an increasingly diffuse global jihadist movement. This global movement consists of numerous groups, in dozens of countries, which are often described as "al-Qaʿida affiliates." For many of these groups, al-Qaʿida serves primarily as a source of ideological inspiration rather than operational guidance or material support. As some observers have put it, in the broad context of the global jihadist activity, al-Qaʿida has been replaced by "al-Qaʿida-ism."[1]

This transformed threat is potentially more dangerous than the one posed by the original al-Qaʿida because, as former White House counterterrorism adviser Richard Clarke has written, it is "simultaneously more decentralized and more radical."[2] Al-Qaʿida has become, in the words of French scholar Gilles Kepel, a "terrorist NGO," without "real estate to be occupied, military hardware to be destroyed, and a regime to be overthrown."[3] A "decapitation" strategy focusing on the elimination of a small group of senior figures in the original al-Qaʿida network is no longer an adequate or appropriate strategy for dealing with a jihadist threat that has, metaphorically speaking, metastasized.

It has also become increasingly clear that the United States is, in many ways, losing the battle for "hearts and minds" in the Arab and Muslim worlds. In the aftermath of the Iraq campaign, Defense Secretary Donald Rumsfeld himself asked, in a leaked October 2003 memo, whether U.S. efforts might in fact be facilitating the enlargement of jihadist ranks. The National Intelligence Council concluded, in a recent unclassified report, that, more than three years into the Bush Administration's war on terror, "the key factors that spawned international terrorism show no signs of abating over the next 15 years…. Foreign jihadists—individuals ready to fight anywhere they believe Muslim lands are under attack by what they see as 'infidel invaders'—enjoy a growing sense of support from Muslims who are not necessarily supporters of terrorism."[4]

Thus, current policy for prosecuting the war on terror is badly in need of repair. A similar imperative for course correction is evident in the Bush Administration's handling of post-Saddam Iraq. The military campaign to unseat Saddam Hussein and establish democratic government in Iraq was the signature foreign-policy initiative of the Administration's first term; it is certainly the most controversial single step taken to date by President Bush and, arguably, the one with the most attendant risks.

As the president enters his second term, many of those risks seem very much in play, and the ultimate outcome of the American effort to lay the

---

1 The National Intelligence Council (NIC) argues that, by 2020, al-Qaʿida "will have been superceded [sic] by similarly inspired but more diffuse Islamic extremist groups." National Intelligence Council, "Mapping the Global Future: Report of the National Intelligence Council's 2020 Project," December 2004, p. 94; available at http://www.cia.gov/nic/NIC_2020_project.html.

2 Richard Clarke, "A War of Ideas," *Washington Post Book World,* November 21, 2004.

3 Gilles Kepel, *The War for Muslim Minds: Islam and the West,* trans. by Pascale Ghazaleh (Harvard University Press, 2004), p. 111.

4 National Intelligence Council, "Mapping the Global Future," p. 94.

foundations for a stable and democratic post-Saddam political order remains very much in doubt. Even supporters of the president's decision to launch Operation Iraqi Freedom, such as Thomas Friedman and William Kristol, have bemoaned what they see as the Administration's serial mistakes in handling the post-conflict period.

The consequences of U.S. policy failure in Iraq would be profound, indeed. Continuing instability in Iraq is already making the country a developmental arena providing "recruitment, training grounds, technical skills and language proficiency for a new class of terrorists"[5]; an Iraq from which the United States had to depart without consolidating minimal order would be even more of a terrorist enclave. An anarchical Iraq would very likely collapse into civil war, threatening the stability of neighboring countries and inviting their intervention. Given these stakes, it is critical that the United States get Iraq right, but that is likely to require some significant departures from the current approach.

As it enters its second term, the Bush Administration must also face up to its lack of an effective strategy for dealing with state sponsors of terror that are simultaneously pursuing WMD capabilities; this deficit is especially problematic with regard to Iran and its nuclear ambitions. During its first term, the president and his senior advisers pursued two alternative approaches to dealing with this kind of "rogue" regime in the context of the war on terror.

To confront the Taliban in Afghanistan and Saddam Hussein in Iraq, the President and his senior advisers opted for a strategy of coercive regime change. In the case of Libya, however, the Administration picked up on a process of conditional engagement with the regime of Mu'ammar al-Qaddafi that had begun during the Clinton Administration. Conditional engagement helped to persuade Libya to meet its international obligations arising from the December 1988 bombing of Pan Am 103 over Lockerbie, Scotland and helped set the stage for successful U.S. engagement with Tripoli over weapons of mass destruction.

The Administration has so far not developed a coherent approach to dealing with other regional rogues—most notably, Iran and Syria. The president and his senior advisers have been loath to engage in a process of conditional engagement with the current regimes in Tehran and Damascus. In the aftermath of the 9/11 attacks, both Iran and Syria sought to cooperate with the United States in various ways, clearly wishing not to get caught on the wrong side of a U.S.-led war on global terrorism. However, the president and his national security team resisted anything more than limited tactical cooperation with these regimes, arguing that broader engagement would be an unwarranted concession and a reward for bad behavior. The Administration's willingness to try conditional engagement with Libya remains, at this point, an exception to its publicly stated reluctance to negotiate the rehabilitation of rogue states.

The Administration has not been able to develop efficacious options for coercing change in problematic Iranian and Syrian behaviors. The ongoing costs—material and otherwise—of U.S. involvement in Iraq mean that the Administration has had no option for pursuing coercive regime change in either Iran or Syria. Similarly, the United States has virtually no options for unilaterally increasing economic pressures on Tehran or Damascus.

Without many coercive unilateral policy options and with the President resistant to engagement

---

5 *Ibid.*

with regimes he considers fundamentally illegitimate, the possibilities for crafting an effective
strategy for dealing with problematic Iranian
and Syrian behaviors were severely limited during the Administration's first term. This must
change, particularly with regard to Iran, if the
United States is to avoid significant reverses in
its regional position during President Bush's
second term.

For other important components of America's
Middle East policy—encouraging Arab-Israeli
peacemaking, for example, or managing important bilateral relationships with key regional
partners such as Egypt and Saudi Arabia—the
Bush Administration's first-term approach is, if
not courting disaster, at least permitting
important U.S. interests to drift in ways that,
over time, could prove strategically dysfunctional. In these areas, as well, the means
by which the Administration pursues its policy
goals must be chosen with a more acute appreciation of the strategic realities facing the
United States

A second assessment shared by the authors of the
essays that follow is that President Bush's emphasis on regional transformation and reform has
been insufficiently nuanced and presented and
pursued in ways that have fostered doubts about
American credibility and raised questions about
the Administration's policy priorities. In Bush's
first term, far-reaching presidential rhetoric
shone a spotlight on the issue of reform, especially political reform. Bush's use of the bully
pulpit placed pressure on Arab regimes to look
responsive and lent a degree of cover to some
Arab activists, but it also produced a certain
degree of backlash in the region.

Unfortunately, the president's high-minded sen-
timents were matched neither by appropriately
large-scale programmatic activities nor by consistent diplomacy. This gap created perceptions,
especially in the region, that the president and his
senior advisers were stymied by the tradeoffs
associated with promoting greater openness in
states where the United States has important
strategic interests and that the ultimate drivers
for U.S. policy remained support for Israel and
narrow economic concerns, with perhaps an
increased admixture of ideological hostility to
Arab and Muslim interests.

Being serious about reform means that the
promotion of positive change and liberalization
must be grounded in an appreciation of the full
range of American interests at stake. There is,
of course, a powerful "realist" argument for
making the promotion of reform a more salient
component of America's Middle East policy. It
is difficult to see how states like Egypt or Saudi
Arabia will be able to sustain their strategic
cooperation with the United States in the
medium-to-long term without recasting the
basic compact between rulers and ruled in
those societies. Within such a realist framework,
the tradeoffs involved in promoting greater
openness can and should be forthrightly
acknowledged.

The example of Algeria's aborted 1992 elections
stands as the nightmare vision for American
policymakers of what democracy might bring to
the Arab world: legitimately elected Islamist
governments that are anti-American, and ultimately anti-democratic, in orientation. More
generally, broad American pressure for political
change may end up being an entry point for
extremism and instability, and may even
increase the likelihood of outcomes that are
detrimental to our interests

In addition, pressuring friendly Arab regimes to
democratize may come at the price of their cooperation on other matters of interest to the United
States. For example, it is certainly true that the
negotiation of peace treaties with Israel would
have been more complicated, perhaps impossible, with democracies in Egypt and Jordan.

Would the United States be able to persuade a fully democratized Egypt or Saudi Arabia to extend the necessary degree of counterterrorism and security cooperation for Washington to prosecute an effective war on terror?

Ultimately, the encouragement of reform in the broader Middle East must be thought through and pursued on a country-by-country basis, with policies developed and tailored to the specific circumstances of each country. Reform may be an imperative for the region, but the manner in which reform is implemented needs to be adapted to the unique circumstances of individual countries and what the United States needs from these countries. In these complex calculations, the avoidance of tradeoffs against near-term U.S. interests should be considered in tandem with an accounting of the medium-to-long term risks of inaction.

This sort of balance eluded the Bush Administration during its first term. Finding it is clearly not an easy task; the authors of the essays that follow are not in complete agreement how to do it, particularly for countries like Egypt and Saudi Arabia with which the United States has long-standing strategic partnerships. Among those addressing aspects of this problem in their essays, Shibley Telhami, James Steinberg, and Flynt Leverett argue that, in such cases, an early emphasis on economic reform, improvement of human rights performance, and guided liberalization in the political sphere is the most effective and prudent course. Tamara Cofman Wittes, on the other hand, argues that such a strategy is insufficient to secure the broad range of U.S. interests in the region; instead, the United States needs to be prepared to apply top-down pressure for broad political liberalization alongside these other efforts. Nevertheless, all the authors agree that the president and his senior advisers need to find the right balance between the near-term costs of encouraging reform and the medium-to-long-term risks of inaction.

Another important assessment linking all of the essays is a sense that not only does the Bush approach to particular components of its Middle East policy have significant deficiencies, but that the president and his senior advisers have compartmentalized these various components in ways that have undercut the overall effectiveness of their policy and weakened the U.S. posture in the region. A number of examples could be adduced to demonstrate this point, but the case of Iraq policy seems particularly apposite. Many commentators have observed that, at this point, the most immediate priority of President Bush's broader Middle East strategy must be Iraq. The Administration must find a way to reduce its burdens in Iraq without paving the way for chaos in that critical country if other parts of the president's Middle East policy are to have a chance of working.

As Iraq has become both a magnet for jihadists who want to fight America and a *cause célèbre* that boosts recruitment and support for extremist groups elsewhere, it is hard to see how the United States can turn the corner in the global war on terror until Iraq has been defused as an issue for Islamic radicals. Furthermore, the current level of American military and logistical commitment in Iraq has reduced the range of actionable policy options for dealing with other problem states in the region, such as Iran. American difficulties in the post-conflict period have also hampered the Administration's efforts to encourage economic and political reform in the region by allowing entrenched regimes to argue that the alternative to authoritarianism is not orderly change but chaotic instability.

Thus, unless the United States stabilizes the situation in Iraq and puts that country on a credible path toward the extension of a legitimate, representative Iraqi government's authority over all Iraq, the chances for achieving anything else in the Middle East will be seriously hampered. But it is equally the case that the prospects for stabilizing Iraq would be significantly enhanced if that objective were made part of a broader regional strategy. In this broader strategy, positive results in other areas would help to reinforce progress in Iraq and vice versa.

To achieve such a symbiosis, the Bush Administration will, in its second term, need to develop an integrated Middle East strategy with at least eight branches:

1. Refocusing the war on terror.

2. Restoring America's standing in the Arab and Muslim worlds.

3. Encouraging political, economic, and social reform in the Arab and Muslim worlds.

4. Promoting a comprehensive Middle East peace (including Syria and Lebanon).

5. Stabilizing Iraq.

6. Denying Iran nuclear weapons and neutralizing its use of terror against peacemaking efforts in the Arab-Israeli arena.

7. Ending Syria's support for terrorism and eliciting greater Syrian cooperation with U.S. regional objectives.

8. Rolling back the jihadist threat in Saudi Arabia and securing America's energy interests in the Persian Gulf.

An integrated approach not only increases the chances of promoting progress on all eight tracks but also improves the prospects for achieving a priority identified during the presidential campaign: strengthening alliances and utilizing them to ease the burden of American leadership. For example, European and Arab leaders all insist that Middle East peacemaking is their priority. By making it one of his, President Bush strengthens his ability to secure their support for his other priorities, especially vis-à-vis Iraq and Iran. Indeed, if the Administration is to succeed with any of its objectives, it will need to make allied cooperation on all of them an essential adjunct to its Middle East strategy.

ALTERNATIVE APPROACHES

Against this backdrop, the authors of the seven essays that follow have sought to craft policy approaches that will be both more effective than current policy at achieving U.S. goals in particular areas and more compatible with an integrated regional strategy. Three of the essays treat issues that cut across the region—the war on terror, Arab-Israeli peacemaking, and promoting reform. Four deal with U.S. policy toward critical countries in the region—Iraq, Iran, Syria, and Saudi Arabia.

The essays begin with an examination of the requirements for a successful campaign against "Binladenism" by Shibley Telhami and James Steinberg. This essay takes as its point of departure the imperative to refocus the war on terror against a more dispersed threat. As Usama bin Laden has become less the leader of a particular organization and more the champion and figurehead for a radical Islamist ideology, it seems appropriate to define the enemy in the war on terror as "Binladenism."

Refocusing the war on terror against Binladenism will entail not only the use of military force, but also the application of all elements of national power—intelligence, law enforcement, economic assistance, diplomacy, and public diplomacy—on a global basis. (It is striking that, in the Bush Administration's 2002 National Security Strategy, the list of elements of national power that must be brought to bear in the war on terror does not include either diplomacy or public diplomacy.) Because of the increasingly devolved nature of the threat, the global counterterrorism campaign is more likely to resemble a war of attrition on multiple fronts than a small number of comparatively surgical strikes against a single adversary.

Telhami and Steinberg argue that mounting this sort of campaign is going to require unprecedented levels of international cooperation, both globally and within the Arab and Muslim worlds. Their strategy focuses on establishing appropriate international and regional contexts for winning the degree of cooperation from other states that the United States needs to prevail in the fight against Binladenism. This approach has significant implications for macro-issues of foreign policy and international organization. It also underscores the importance of the way in which the United States conditions the regional context in the broader Middle East for its foreign-policy initiatives and pursues the battle for "hearts and minds" in the Arab and Muslim worlds.

Arguably, there is nothing more essential to building greater international and regional support for U.S. policy objectives and creating a more positive climate in the Arab and Muslim worlds for U.S. policy initiatives than more robust and effective U.S. engagement in Arab-Israeli peacemaking. As Telhami and Steinberg point out, the Arab-Israeli conflict has become the "prism of pain" through which most Arabs evaluate U.S. policy. Because of the centrality of this conflict to almost everything that the United States wants to accomplish in the broader Middle East, the second essay, by Martin Indyk, looks at the opportunities and risks for the Bush Administration in the Arab-Israeli arena.

For Indyk, successful U.S. engagement in promoting a final settlement to the Israeli-Palestinian conflict will require two things. First, the United States (and other international and regional players) will need to work hard to bolster a moderate, post-Arafat Palestinian leadership, through the holding of Palestinian elections, efforts to rebuild Palestinian capacity for governance, and the successful implementation of Prime Minister Sharon's Gaza disengagement initiative. Second, the United States should, relatively early in the process, lay out a fuller vision for the "end game"—that is, the parameters for negotiating final-status issues, including borders, Jerusalem, and refugees—than the Bush Administration has heretofore been willing to offer. This is needed both to support the consolidation of a moderate Palestinian leadership and to lay the groundwork for a renewed political process.

Indyk lays out a comprehensive strategy for accomplishing these two steps, including recommendations on modalities (such as the appointment of a presidential envoy) and for the timing of specific initiatives. Beyond the Palestinian track, Indyk believes that the Bush Administration should also pay more attention to the possibility of reviving an Israeli-Syrian negotiating track than it did during its first term in office.

The third essay, by Tamara Cofman Wittes, deals with the promotion of reform in the Arab and Muslim worlds. Wittes makes a strong, interest-based argument for a forward-leaning American posture on both economic and political reform. In making concrete policy recommendations, she argues for a clear distinction between relatively urgent policy goals and goals that can prudently be achieved only on a gradual basis. She further lays out a framework identifying where to focus American efforts, and discusses how to handle the inevitable tradeoffs entailed in a policy of promoting reform.

The fourth essay, by Kenneth Pollack, treats the most immediately pressing foreign policy problem that President Bush faces in his second term—namely, the challenge of stabilizing post-Saddam Iraq. Pollack—an articulate prewar champion of coercive regime change in Iraq—argues for a fundamental shift in the U.S. approach to reconstruction and political reconstitution there if the Bush Administration is to avoid a major policy failure.

More specifically, rather than continue down the path of post-conflict stabilization—which may have made sense in theory as the optimal approach for the United States in a post-Saddam environment, but which has been rendered unworkable by the unwillingness of the Administration to commit sufficient manpower and resources to secure all of Iraq—the president and his senior advisers need to move rapidly toward a genuine counterinsurgency strategy. This would mean not just a dramatic adjustment in the way that U.S. forces deploy and conduct themselves on the ground—focusing on creating enclaves in particular regions and slowly expanding outward, as opposed to trying to control the entire country—but also a radical change in the direction of economic reconstruction and political reconstitution.

The fifth and sixth essays, by Kenneth Pollack and Flynt Leverett, respectively, consider how the Bush Administration might deal more effectively with the two outstanding rogue states that Washington currently faces in the region: Iran and Syria. It is an open question whether the Bush Administration in its second term can develop workable strategies for getting Iran and Syria out of the terrorism business, rolling back (especially in the case of Iran) the WMD threats posed by these states, and enlisting their support for U.S. objectives in the region and in the struggle against violent jihadists. Neither Pollack nor Leverett believes that a strategy of coercive regime change, applied to Iran or Syria, would serve U.S. interests. Instead, accomplishing these goals is likely to require a fundamental shift in the Administration's reluctance to engage regimes it considers, in many ways, morally illegitimate.

Pollack argues that the United States should be willing to pursue a "grand bargain" with the current leadership of the Islamic Republic if that proves possible, but should develop an alternative posture of "carrots-and-sticks" engagement with Tehran in order to induce modifications in problematic Iranian behaviors. Leverett argues that the United States can achieve a number of its most important policy goals toward Syria through a strategy of hard-nosed, "carrots-and-sticks" engagement with Damascus.

The final essay, also by Flynt Leverett, examines the challenges facing President Bush in managing America's critical bilateral relationship with Saudi Arabia. Saudi Arabia is, truly, "ground zero" in the war on terror and remains indispensable to America's energy security for the foreseeable future. Unfortunately, since the September 11 attacks, the U.S.-Saudi relationship has gone through unprecedented strains. On both sides, voices arguing for a retrenchment in the two countries' sixty-year strategic partnership are more prominent than ever before. Given the imperative of Saudi support for key U.S. policy objectives and the importance of preserving the kingdom's long-term stability, the United States needs a strategy for dealing with Riyadh that improves the level of Saudi cooperation on important regional and energy issues while simultaneously encouraging genuine (if incremental) liberalization in the kingdom. In his first term, though, President Bush effectively left the U.S.-Saudi partnership drifting in post-9/11 winds. Leverett argues that the best way to reinvigorate this partnership is by combining more intensive bilateral engagement with the Saudi leadership with the establishment of a regional security framework for the Persian Gulf.

Thus, these essays seek to lay out alternative approaches to achieving the broad range of U.S. policy goals in the Middle East. The authors hope that, taken together, the essays also provide the elements for a genuinely integrated strategic framework that will help decisionmakers manage both the changes and the continuities in America's post-9/11 Middle East policy. The absence of such a framework in the past four years has weakened the efficacy of American foreign policy during a critically challenging time for U.S. interests. Hopefully, an informed discussion of policy alternatives may produce more satisfying outcomes during the next four years.

Fighting Binladenism

Shibley Telhami and James Steinberg

As the Bush Administration begins its second term, it faces the challenge of refocusing the global war on terror. The war on terror was originally presented, to American and foreign audiences, as the overarching framework for American foreign and national security policy in the post-9/11 world. However, as a conceptual and rhetorical device, it has become less useful (and potentially counterproductive) for this purpose as ever more diverse policy goals have been placed under its rubric and as its international legitimacy has declined following the intervention in Iraq. If these trends are not corrected in President Bush's second term, there is a significant probability that the "war on terror" will ultimately become little more than a slogan to justify other foreign policy objectives and not a rallying point for gaining international support for U.S. actions.

Under current circumstances, refocusing the war on terror will necessarily entail two related shifts in U.S. policy. First, the definition of the objective of the war on terror has become too vague, making it imperative to specify more clearly the nature of the threat. Of course, the United States, as a matter of policy, opposes all terrorism, defined as the deliberate targeting of non-combatants for political purposes. But the threat to U.S. interests that emerged in such a high-profile fashion on September 11, 2001 is characterized not simply by means that a range of groups around the world employ, but also by a particular complex of aims, capabilities, and lack of responsiveness to traditional deterrence strategies.

By these criteria, America's primary enemy in the post-9/11 world is most appropriately identified, not as "terrorism" in a generic sense, but as "Binladenism."

- Obviously, Binladenism refers to al-Qaʻida; the term also refers to other groups that have come to embrace al-Qaʻida's mission. From a strategic perspective, Binladenism is an international movement that aims to establish a puritanical Islamic order throughout the Arab and Muslim worlds, sees the United States as its principal enemy, and is empowered by transnational capabilities and a willingness to use any means available.

- Although Binladenism takes its name from the founder of al-Qaʻida, its orbit extends well beyond the limits of the al-Qaʻida organization and it almost certainly would survive the passing of Usama bin Laden himself.[1]

Second, the president and his senior advisers need to acknowledge that, to be effective in confronting, isolating, and weakening the Binladenist threat, their efforts will depend, in large part, on garnering maximal international cooperation and winning allies in Muslim countries themselves.

- This means that, in order to succeed, the Administration's strategy for a refocused war on Binladenism must be devised with a clear understanding of the international and regional environments in which that strategy will be implemented.

- What is needed is a broad-based effort to shape international and regional contexts for the war on Binladenism that would be more conducive to securing sustained international and regional cooperation.

THE GLOBAL CONTEXT

Understanding the global context for U.S. foreign policy as President Bush enters his second term must start with the recognition that traditional respect for and acceptance of notions of America's "global leadership" and standing as the "indispensable nation" are being called into serious question by large segments of the international community. To be sure, much of the current international resentment of the United States is driven by the Bush Administration's approach to foreign policy, which sees America alone as the arbiter of what is good for the world. However, the United States must come to grips with a more basic loss of faith by key international actors, not only in the Bush Administration and its policies, but in a post-Cold War international order that has proven insufficiently protective of those actors' interests.

Many countries were profoundly shaken by an American assertion of unilateral power after 9/11 in ways that went against their perceived vital interests. Regardless of the course of U.S. policy during the next presidential term—whether in relation to the war on terrorism, the proliferation of weapons of mass destruction, or other important problems such as the rise of China—it is clear that the way in which Washington has asserted American hegemony has itself, in many situations, become a factor limiting the degree of cooperation that the United States can elicit from other key countries.

It is hard to see how the United States can establish an optimal international context for the war on Binladenism if it does not address this concern.

- It is clear, for example, that one important factor in the reluctance of Europeans and others to help the United States succeed after the Iraq war was based on the fear that an American "success" in a war they largely opposed would further empower American foreign policies in ways that these other countries would consider threatening.

- In general, states worry more or less about the power of others depending on how that power is used. Thus, some of the international concern about President Bush's unilateralism could be addressed by a modification of his foreign policy. But this probably will not suffice given the inevitable concern that the United States could change course again, after another

---

1 The term Binladenism seems not only analytically useful, but also tactically preferable as a label for America's enemies in the war on terror, at least in terms of how it would be received in Muslim countries. Alternatives such as "international *jihadists*" are potentially counterproductive. Most Islamist moderates accept the theological notion of *jihad* but interpret it in non-violent ways. If the United States aims to win these moderates, Washington must label its enemies in ways that do not appear aimed at the Muslim world's moderate majorities, even in name.

electoral cycle or some other domestic political development.

This suggests that something more profound than short-term adjustments in particular policies or tactical approaches will be required to secure long-term international cooperation on matters central to U.S. interests, including terrorism. Even as the United States sets fighting terrorism as its global priority, each international actor has its own priorities. Winning the cooperation of those states whose support is critical to the ultimate success of the war on terror will require the United States to show greater attention to the vital interests of those states.

In particular, the United States needs to focus on the key actors whose help will be essential for global policies on core American post-9/11 concerns—in particular, terrorism and nuclear proliferation.

- These actors include China, Russia, the United Kingdom, Germany, France, and Japan among the world's more powerful states.

- They include Egypt, Indonesia, Pakistan, Saudi Arabia, and Turkey among Muslim countries, and Brazil and India among non-Muslim Third World countries.

These are the critical players who have levers of their own and whose policies will affect America's degree of success in implementing its policies. Regarding each one of these countries, U.S. policymakers should ask the following question: What are their foreign policy/national security priorities? What actions can we take to signal our responsiveness to their vital interests in order to secure their sustained cooperation with ours? This may in the end be very difficult as some interests will inevitably conflict, but the mere openness to this approach will generate far more short-term cooperation than is now available.

These bilateral arrangements will be helpful but not sufficient. The issues on the table today pertain to the very global order in the coming decade and the role of the United States in that order.

And, here, there is an extraordinary opportunity for the Bush Administration: just at a time when global concern is focused on perceived U.S. disregard for international institutions, the early months of President Bush's second term could be used to launch a new initiative to strengthen and revise international institutions, including the United Nations, World Bank, and International Monetary Fund. In the case of Germany and Japan among the OECD countries and developing countries such as India and Brazil, a more prominent role in these institutions would have to be considered, including the possible restructuring of the UN Security Council.

- The United States is likely to face increasing pressure on these questions; if the Bush Administration resists, it will be undermining prospects for essential international cooperation with its key policies.

- If, on the other hand, the Bush Administration initiated a broad dialogue on the future of international institutions, it could put forth specific demands: in particular, shifting burden sharing away from the United States and insisting on stronger international rules on terrorism, weapons proliferation, and human rights.

Such an initiative would, at a minimum, change the nature of the current international debate over U.S. foreign policy; more ambitiously, it might actually invigorate international institutions in ways that increased the degree of international cooperation on matters related to American vital interests. The recent report of the UN Secretary General's High Level Panel on Threats, Challenges, and Change offers a path forward—with its unequivocal rejection of terrorism in all its forms and recognition of the need under some circumstances to act preemptively—in the context of a global security system that recognizes the importance of responding to the full range of threats to security.

THE REGIONAL CONTEXT

In the war against Binladenism, the United States obviously must seek to destroy the movement when and where this is possible. But a counter-terrorism model that envisions only the movement's eradication through the direct action of the United States and its allies is too limited for the task at hand. American strategy must also seek to isolate and weaken the movement—to render it ineffective.

To do this, the United States must differentiate between Binladenism and rising Islamic nationalism in those countries that Binladenism targets for recruitment. U.S. policymakers must learn from America's mistakes in the first two decades of the Cold War, when the United States failed to differentiate between anti-imperial nationalism and communism, and between ideology and state interests, with the costs of unnecessary wars such as Vietnam and the failure to recognize early on the emerging Sino-Soviet split.

It is clear that the vast majority of people in Arab and Muslim countries resent the United States not because they share the goals of Binladenism, but because of a rising tide of Islamic, anti-imperial nationalism that transcends local concerns. This particular form of nationalism is a function of both contemporary perceptions of U.S. foreign policy and the perceived failures of Arab and Muslim states and of secular nationalism.

The result is a complex set of perceptions, which are troublesome but not fatal to a well conceived effort to establish effective cooperation in the fight against Binladenism.

- In 2000, for example, more than 60 percent of Saudis expressed confidence in the United States; today less than 4 percent do so.

- In 2001, most people in the Arab world highlighted their Arab identity in describing themselves; today most highlight their Islamic identity.

- Most Arabs today have a more favorable view of al-Qaʿida than of the United States. Yet it is clear that their negative view of the United States is what is driving their positive image of al-Qaʿida, not the other way around. The vast majority of Arabs and Muslims reject the puritanical world al-Qaʿida seeks: Most of them rejected the Taliban world, and most, for example, want women to work outside the home.

- Even as they express the rising importance of their Islamic identity, they choose non-Islamic leaders as their favorites: In a survey conducted during the summer of 2003, the three most popular leaders in the Arab world were Gamal Abd al-Nasir (dead since 1970, before the vast majority of Arabs living were born!), Jacques Chirac, and Saddam Hussein. The only thing these leaders share is perceived defiance of the United States.

Thus, for the majority of Muslims, attitudes toward the United States reflect resentment of American policies, not love for Binladenism. Against this backdrop, an effective U.S. strategy for fighting Binladenism must reduce the anger and anti-American sentiment of this Arab and Muslim majority. At a minimum, U.S. policy must assure that these populations are not tempted to support Binladenism in a conflict with the United States that would be far too costly and unpredictable.

Especially in the Arab world, the rise of Islamic nationalism is also driven by a perceived failure of states and secular Arab nationalism to address the pervasive sense of powerlessness. In many countries, Islamists have sought to address this sense of powerlessness by establishing grassroots connections to society, including by providing badly needed services that no other actors are providing.

If the United States is to be more effective in battling Islamists for hearts and minds in the broader Middle East, U.S. policy needs to compete with radical Islamism in addressing this sense of powerlessness. Reducing Arab and Muslim anger at the United States and addressing pervasive perceptions of powerlessness will require American engagement on the core issues that matter most to Arabs and Muslims around the world. These include U.S. support for authoritarianism, the war in Iraq, and Arab-Israeli issues.

While all of these are important, especially in the Arab world, nothing is more central than the Israeli-Palestinian conflict, which remains the lens through which most Arabs see the United States and interpret the intentions of our policies.

- In the last three years, as General Musharraf recently pointed out, this issue has become central even in non-Arab Muslim countries, such as Pakistan, Turkey, and Indonesia. In the same way that the September 11 attacks have become America's "prism of pain" through which many Americans view the Muslim world (and suicide bombings have become the new prism of pain for many Israelis, in addition to the Holocaust), the Palestinian issue is central to most Arabs and Muslims.

- In that regard, the most important signal the Bush Administration could send to gain the attention of the region is to revive hope for the peaceful resolution of the Israeli-Palestinian conflict, consistent with continued U.S. support for Israeli security.

Advocating democracy is something that the United States should do as an end in itself, as a reflection of core American values, and as something that the region would in the end benefit from even more than we will. While democratization is essential in the long term to countering Binladenism, it is more complicated in the short and medium term. U.S. policymakers should be careful because the expectations raised could be unrealistic and their lack of fulfillment counterproductive for U.S. policy goals—a danger that could be exacerbated by the president's sweeping assertions in his second inaugural address. There are three reasons for concern:

First, the sort of terrorism that most threatens the United States (with transnational capabilities and a degree of independence from states) thrives where there is maximal instability.

- In the literature on transitions to democracy, where there is little consensus on how to make such transitions successfully, there is one clear conclusion: transitions are highly unstable and unpredictable, and successful ones take a long time.

- Thus, Iraq may yet become a democracy, but in the foreseeable future it will remain unstable, and thus more hospitable to terrorists than it was under the dictatorship of Saddam Hussein, as the National Intelligence Council's "Mapping the Global Future" report recently concluded.[2]

For this reason, the United States will almost always face tradeoffs in pursuing the war on Binladenism as a national priority.

- In Pakistan, for example, the difficulty is evident: the United States needs General Musharraf to deal relentlessly with al-Qa'ida

---

2 National Intelligence Council, "Mapping the Global Future: Report of the National Intelligence Council's 2020 Project," December 2004; available at http://www.cia.gov/nic/NIC_2020_project.html.

and its supporters in the near term just as we need him to open up Pakistan's political system as an antidote to radicalism in the long term.

- In Iraq, the United States faces the immediate need for security and stability through a strong government in Baghdad, yet we will ultimately fail if Shi'ite majoritarianism replaces Ba'athist authoritarianism instead of an effective pluralist form of governance.

The gap between aspirational rhetoric and strategic reality is not lost on most people in the region. As noted in the Introduction, this gap engenders perceptions in the region of American insincerity, even hypocrisy. This is hardly conducive to the establishment of a regional context for a more effective war on Binladenism.

Second, the Bush Administration faces a structural problem in the short-to-medium term in its advocacy of democracy as part of the war on terror: the Arab and Muslim publics that the Administration would like to empower are far more hostile to the United States than the current (largely authoritarian) governments.

- This is especially evident in the gap between publics and governments on matters related to the Iraq war. Majorities in the Arab world do not believe that the United States seeks to spread democracy; most say that the Middle East is less democratic than it was before the Iraq war, which was in part aimed to spread democracy.

- This particular problem suggests that American foreign policy must reach out to publics and civil society in the Arab and Muslim worlds as a precondition for a broader strategy of promoting political reform.

Third, the United States cannot impose democracy alone, especially if there are too many actors resisting its efforts in the region and whose cooperation is needed to fight Binladenism. The Bush Administration needs the largest possible coalitions of publics and governments to marginalize the extremists—even those who do not share our view of democracy should be included.

All of this does not mean that the Bush Administration should abandon the objective of reform—the status quo is simply not sustainable. It does mean that the Administration needs to find a way to work with its regional partners— that are cooperating with us in the fight against Binladenism—to push for economic and political reform in ways that do not undermine that support. This suggests a three pronged approach:

- emphasize issues of human rights, on which there is broad international support;

- emphasize economic reform, on which there are incentives for governments and the private sector to cooperate and which almost always translates into public demand for political empowerment, over political reform; and

- seek more direct ways to empower civil society.

Above all, except in the case of human rights, where results should be immediate, look for long-term progressive change, not immediate transformations. This nuanced strategy will allow the United States to create a climate of cooperation in both the short and long term that is essential to securing the nation against the most powerful threat now facing it.

Promoting Reform in the Arab World: A Sustainable Strategy

Tamara Cofman Wittes

President Bush's "forward strategy of freedom" was a bold restatement of American interests in the Arab Middle East, but it requires a bold and calculated restructuring of American policy to match. The question we face today is how to reorient our policy tools and our relationships with international and regional partners so as to institutionalize what is often described as a generational effort. Building a sustainable and successful policy requires finding an appropriate balance among our sometimes conflicting interests, setting priorities to help meet both urgent requirements of the war on terror as well as longer-term goals, and devising means to minimize the risks inherent in such an ambitious, and necessary, shift in U.S. policy. Properly calibrating our policy initiatives also requires a clear understanding of the regional dynamics influencing reform, and a recognition of how the United States can most effectively influence an ongoing process of Arab political, social, and economic change.

The Vanishing Status Quo

America's core objective in the Middle East has been and remains regional stability. Stability in the Middle East is necessary to ensure the free flow of energy supplies to world markets, to facil-itate our naval traffic from the Mediterranean to the Indian Ocean, and to protect the security of Israel. For six decades, America's interest in a stable Middle Eastern region was, by and large, well served by our support of status-quo Arab regimes, including most prominently the Saudi dynasty, Jordan under the late King Hussein and his son King Abdullah II, and Egypt under Anwar Sadat and his successor, Hosni Mubarak.

The primary threat to Middle East stability in the years to come, however, emanates from the combination of demographic expansion, economic stagnation, and political alienation that together present an intense and increasing challenge to the legitimacy and governability of key Arab states. Current levels of economic growth are insufficient to create the large number of jobs necessary to absorb the Arab world's overwhelmingly young population as it enters the job market in the coming ten years. Regimes whose legitimacy rested on postcolonial Arab nationalism, tribal loyalties, or generous, oil-fed social welfare systems feel all of these foundations undermined by local and global trends of the past decade. Regimes that have relied on a combination of ideology, statism, external security threats, and repression to sustain themselves in power are reaching the limits of their ability to buy off or

deflect popular dissent, while increased aware-
ness among Arab citizens of international trends
and frustration at internal stagnation—and,
more recently, President Bush's own rhetoric—
have provoked a wave of introspection and rising
demands for change.

Because of these developments, Arab elites and
political leaders have renewed their discussion of
the need for change. In response to internal
pressures as well as President Bush's emphasis on
expanding freedom, even the calcified Arab
League issued a declaration supporting vague
and limited reforms, while several non-governmental meetings have produced bold agendas for
political, social, and economic change. The status
quo America has long protected in the Arab
world appears increasingly unsustainable, and
the social and political relationships that have
defined Arab politics since World War II are not
likely to survive the current ferment unchanged.

Building a new social contract between Arab
governments and their citizens is necessary for
the development of a new equilibrium in Arab
regional politics—and for continued fruitful
cooperation between Arab governments and the
United States on key regional challenges including stabilizing Iraq, confronting Iran's nuclear
weapons development, and promoting Arab-
Israeli peace. If Arab governments cannot sustain
the support of their citizens, they will not be able
easily or reliably to work with us on issues of
common concern.

ARAB REFORM AND THE
WAR ON TERROR

America's interest in promoting reform in the
Arab world emanates not only from its long-
standing interest in regional stability, but also
from the newer imperative of the struggle against
Islamist terrorism. The growing social pressures
in the Arab world produce not only a governance
challenge to important U.S. partners, but also a

more direct challenge to the United States. The
disaffected, un- and under-employed youthful
populations that are growing across the Arab
world present sizeable and easy prey for extremist movements—and attempts by some Arab
governments to manage their internal challenges
through repression of Islamist critics or by
encouraging emigration by dissidents can sometimes exacerbate the problem of Islamist extremism elsewhere in the region. A key element of a
successful war on terrorism will be the ability to
marginalize Binladenism within the Arab world
by limiting its appeal—by promoting critical
thinking, pluralism, toleration, and a sense of
forward progress.

While undermining the ability of extremist
ideologies to find mass support is a long-term
project, there are also short-term gains for the
United States in pursuing Arab social, economic,
and political reform. The outcome of the process
of change already underway in the Arab world
is not clear, and the path may not be smooth.
As Arab regimes struggle with their mounting
social, economic, and political challenges, the
results may include repression, civil strife, or
even popular overthrow of friendly regimes. As
governments seek new foundations for legitimacy,
Islamist political discourse may become even
more common and accepted. Any of these trends
would facilitate the activities of Binladenist
groups by opening new arenas for action, reinforcing ideological messages, and eroding local
governability.

American engagement to push reform in the
direction of liberal democracy can help reduce
the risk that the current and coming upheavals
in Arab politics might provide Binladenist ideas
strong new footholds in major countries. The
triumph of radical Islamism in newly open
Arab political competitions is by no means a
foregone conclusion—but it is far more likely if
we do not work to promote liberal alternatives
and to encourage the building of a sound

liberal foundation on which political competition can take place.

THE GOALS OF A PRO-REFORM STRATEGY

America's role in promoting Arab reform is complicated by several factors, including our past history of supporting Arab autocrats, the difficulties attending Iraq's reconstruction, and our widely resented attitudes toward promoting an Israeli-Palestinian accord. Despite these apparent handicaps, the United States has a uniquely important role to play in ensuring the development of a more peaceful, prosperous, and democratic Arab future. The United States, regardless of its reputation in the region, remains the primary military, economic, and cultural influence on Arab states and societies. Ongoing American involvement in the region is a foregone conclusion—therefore, the question is not *whether* U.S. actions ought to impact Arab political development, but *in what way.*

The basic strategy for the United States in promoting democratic change in most Arab states must be an engagement strategy. We are not interested in fomenting popular revolutions in most Arab states (even if we could) and we cannot, for practical reasons, align ourselves wholly with dissident activists (who right now are marginal anyway) against regimes with whom we must continue to interact on other critical issues, such as the Arab-Israeli peace process and counterterrorism.

At the same time, our strategy must be directed at democratic reform, not just regime-guided, limited liberalization, which is the chosen strategy of most Arab regimes today, and to which we are largely acquiescing in our current policy. Although the spectrum of their attitudes is wide, most of the 22 Arab states themselves recognize their looming challenges, and seek to reform in

ways that improve government and economic performance without changing the distribution of political power. While a few forward-leaning regimes have placed limited power in the hands of their peoples through constitutional and electoral reforms, many others are focused instead on cosmetic improvements. The liberalization programs currently embraced by many Arab regimes are not intended, from their viewpoint, to lead to real political competition, but to create an impression of progress and perhaps enhanced prosperity, and thereby to mitigate demands among the public for broader political change.[1]

Limited liberalization, however, is insufficient to secure America's interest in marginalizing extremism and promoting long-term stability, because it entrenches instead of erodes the privileged position of Islamist radicals as the primary popular opponents to existing Arab regimes, and because it will not fully meet the expectations of Arab citizens. These problems are examined in detail in the section below, entitled "A Comprehensive Strategy for Reform." At best, limited liberalization may prolong the lifespan in power of unpopular, autocratic leaders whose legitimacy will remain fragile. At worst, this approach will enhance Islamists' dominance of the opposition ground, expanding the market for Binladenist ideas, while associating us ever more closely with autocratic rulers in an alliance against their citizens' legitimate aspirations for change.

Because American interests in Arab political development dictate broad-reaching goals that diverge from the chosen path of most of our regional allies, our strategy must exert pressures on them to change their policies while minimizing the costs and risks associated with a more aggressive approach. *Our strategy must be to alter the environment within*

---

1 See Daniel Brumberg, "Liberalization Versus Democracy: Understanding Arab Political Reform," Carnegie Endowment for International Peace Working Paper #37 (Washington: Carnegie Endowment, May 2003).

which Arab leaders make decisions about reform, to sharpen the discomfort and increase the costs associated with maintaining the status quo, and to maximize the payoff to them for moving toward more liberal economics, politics, and society.

ASSESSING THE RISKS OF A PRO-REFORM POLICY

To be sure, a policy of promoting political, economic, and social reform in the Arab world carries risks for the United States. Primary among these risks is that pressuring longstanding autocratic regimes to relax their control over political power may produce crisis and chaotic outcomes rather than gradual transitions to democracy. This risk is worth considering, but must be evaluated relative to the risks of instability that accompany a policy of favoring the status quo. If the socioeconomic situation in countries such as Egypt and Saudi Arabia suggests the necessity either of revising the social contract that has long undergirded these autocratic regimes, or of resorting to repression to squelch growing popular discontent, then turmoil is a risk regardless of U.S. attitudes. Given this, it appears preferable to support changes that will facilitate long-term stability, political moderation, and prosperity rather than to continue or even enhance America's already much-resented association with governments whose ability to deliver effectively in response to public needs is increasingly judged a failure by their own citizens.

A further important risk of a pro-reform policy is that democratizing Arab polities might put into power Islamist or otherwise hostile parties. The problem of "one person, one vote, one time," encapsulated in Algeria's experience of Islamist victory, military coup, and civil war, has crystallized as the nightmare vision for American policymakers of what democracy might bring to the Arab world: legitimately elected Islamist governments that are anti-American, and ultimately anti-democratic, in orientation.

It is certainly true in nearly all Arab states today that the largest political opposition is Islamist in character. However, the Islamist advantage evident in many Arab societies today exists at least in part because of the state's long-standing intolerance of social organizations outside the framework of religion and, in some cases, because of the Islamicization of public discourse encouraged by the state in its attempts to co-opt religious elites. Moreover, the region's experience with Islamist parties has moved beyond the experience of Algeria in 1991, and few Islamist parties today can sustain either the mystique or the simplistic sloganeering that swept the FIS to victory.

As a result, it is not clear in many cases whether a more open political process (especially one gradually introduced) would necessarily bring Islamist forces commanding majorities, or whether a more diverse marketplace of ideas and meaningful contestation would reduce the grassroots popularity of Islamist movements to manageable levels. In the Palestinian Authority, where Islamist movements have long held sway as a popular opposition, and where socioeconomic misery and popular dissatisfaction with the party in power are extreme, one might expect overwhelming votes for Islamists. But the first round of municipal elections gave Islamist candidates only one-third of the seats on town councils, and even their Gaza strongholds did not give them unanimous support (although they did receive two-thirds of the vote there). This suggests that the common perception of overwhelming support for Islamist politics is at least in part an artifact of the lack of political freedom. Moreover, it is not clear whether those Islamist forces that could meet with success in an open political process that is itself embedded in a broader system of liberal political rights would necessarily present a threat to American interests in the Middle East. The choice of participation in a rules-based competition might itself help to eliminate the most radical voices from the system.

There remains the question of whether democratic elections are likely to bring to power, if not Islamist leaders, anti-American ones—reflecting the widespread public resentment of U.S. policy evident in many polls of the Arab public. How much damage might democratic, anti-American leaders do to American interests in the Middle East? It is worth remembering that Arab democratization is driven by internal pressures related to socioeconomic demands. Any elected and accountable government would need to maintain reasonable working ties with Europe and the United States in order to accrue much-needed domestic economic growth to satisfy these internal demands. As a result, the logic of cooperation with America on key issues—say, Arab-Israeli peace for Egypt or energy stability and Gulf security for Saudi Arabia—would remain strong.[2] Moreover, there are practical limits on the actions that nationalist successor governments could take that would directly harm American interests in the region. For example, would an elected nationalist or Islamist government in Egypt renounce the 1979 Camp David Accords? It is entirely conceivable that such a government might disrupt formal diplomatic relations with Israel, but it would not have the military capability to initiate conflict—nor indeed, an interest in doing so, since Camp David restored Egyptian territory that would likely be lost again in a new war.

Clearly, though, any American strategy for reform should be formulated to reduce the likelihood of electoral victory by radical Islamist forces, and to limit the potential impact of future Islamist (or other successor) governments on America's regional priorities. How to achieve these objectives will be discussed below, in the section entitled "Hedging Against Risk."

An assertive pro-reform American policy might also risk eroding the cooperation of existing Arab governments with other valuable regional goals. Pressing for democratic transformation in rogue states like Libya or Syria is easy enough; there is little to lose by trying. But the Middle East is full of regimes with which America has worked closely for years and whose cooperation it desires on a variety of security and economic issues, notably including the war on terrorism. Although at times reform incentives can be linked positively to other regional policies (as, for example, in the case of free-trade Qualified Industrial Zones between Egypt, Israel, and the United States), more often achieving a local government's acquiescence to internal reforms will present a tradeoff for the United States with achieving that government's support for other U.S. policy goals. Any American pro-reform policy must therefore be carefully constructed to minimize tradeoffs with, and to create continued positive incentives for, continued cooperation on counterterrorism, Arab-Israeli peace, Iraqi stabilization, and other valued regional initiatives.

THE NEED FOR A COMPREHENSIVE APPROACH TO REFORM

In light of the risks attending a pro-reform policy, it is tempting to embrace an approach to Arab reform that is mainly designed to minimize risk. Three main options are presented in this regard:

- The United States could support Arab regimes' efforts at gradual, limited liberalization as a way of avoiding confrontation with valued regional partners and addressing the perception that we are imposing an agenda on the region.

---

2 Obviously this might not hold true for a revolutionary government, as proved to be the case in post-1979 Iran. The Iranian case is unique for the direct CIA and other American support for the Shah's regime against internal challenges, and in President Carter's sudden abandonment of the Shah without embracing a democratic (or any) alternative. If the Iranian experience offers any lessons for today, it provides all the more reason to promote democratic transformation actively and holistically, rather than to take limited steps toward liberalization that enable the expression of popular frustration without cultivating positive alternatives to the status-quo autocratic regimes. A more tentative approach, ironically, would only make a revolutionary outcome more likely.

- The United States could prioritize economic reforms as more urgent than political reforms (and far less controversial), viewing increased prosperity as both a prerequisite and a catalyst for democratic development.

- To ensure that democratic development goes smoothly, the United States could focus on developing Arab civil society before pressuring Arab governments to share power.

But less ambitious or less confrontational approaches to promoting Arab reform are unlikely to be effective, and may indeed reinforce existing problems in the region that threaten America's interests.

A gradualist strategy carries with it particular dangers for the United States. The liberalization programs currently embraced by many Arab regimes are not intended, from their viewpoint, to lead to real political competition, but to create an impression of progress along with increased prosperity, and thereby to mitigate demands among the public for broader political change. America's embrace of a gradualist strategy assumes that, over time, liberalization will take on such momentum that autocratic Arab regimes will no longer be able to avoid real devolution of power. That is an uncertain assumption: if the regimes lose control, the outcome might be chaotic, and there is no guarantee that the region's long-suppressed liberals will win out. Therefore, we cannot remain agnostic on our desires regarding the end-stage of political reform—we must emphasize and act upon our desire to see democratic rules and political rights prevail.

But the bigger risk in a gradualist strategy is not dramatic change; it is the absence of change. By design, the regimes' top-down liberalization does not relax state control sufficiently to enable the formation of any organized political alternative to the state itself or the Islamist opposition movements. The Islamists have the mosque as a place to organize, while other arenas of social organization are still tightly restricted. In this way, the regimes maintain control—and also maintain the Islamist opposition as the only alternative to their rule. The Islamists' dominance of the opposition is the excuse many regimes use to Washington for why truly free politics is too dangerous and why political reform can go only so far and no farther. The more the Algeria scenario looms in American policymakers' minds as the nightmare to be avoided at all costs, the more our policy falls prey to this cynical strategy by Arab regimes to distort reform to serve their own ends.

Worse still is that America's fear of another Algeria might well be a self-fulfilling prophecy. That's because the longer the U.S. government rewards regimes that "liberalize" without allowing new political forces to develop, the more the Islamists benefit from such limited political openings as do exist. The more entrenched the Islamists become as the political alternative to the status quo, the more the language of Islamism becomes the language of protest politics and other voices become marginalized. The net effect of controlled "liberalization," then, may be not to drain the swamp of extremism, but to expand it. And if liberalization becomes perceived by Arab citizens to be a minimalist sham, or if it is quickly reversed in the wake of public demands for more, then the United States becomes as associated with the subsequent repression and reversal as it may have been with the prior opening.

An economics-driven reform strategy is also insufficient to achieve American goals—and past experience has suggested that it has real limitations when applied to the Arab world. Both the United States (through the "Gore-Mubarak" dialogue with Egypt) and the European Union (through its "Barcelona" process of Euro-Mediterranean dialogue) gave priority to structural economic reforms in key Arab states in the 1990s as a way of reducing state control over economic resources, building trade ties, and creating independent constituents for pro-Western, pro-reform policies by Arab nationalist regimes.

But in most Arab states, state control over economic benefits—not just state-owned industry and civil-sector employment, but government controls on trade and taxes, corrupt contracting, and selective rule enforcement—all serve to ensure the loyalty of even the private sector to the ruling regime or family. As a result, structural economic reforms that are necessary to facilitate international trade, attract foreign investment, or otherwise produce long-term economic growth also tend to undermine the economic foundations of political support for the ruling authority. Hence, Egyptian economic reforms ground to a halt in the 1990s when the political costs of economic change began to mount. And because of the dependence of private sector actors on the beneficence of overwhelming government authority, Tunisia's impressive economic growth and jolt of foreign investment have not loosened the grip of one of the region's most effective police states.[3] The lesson of the 1990s is that, unless political liberalization and economic reforms are undertaken in tandem, there is no compelling reason to expect that the latter will provoke the former.[4] Indeed, their past experience leads some Egyptian reformers to suggest that, in the absence of accompanying political liberalization to enable debate of economic policy and to provide alternative sources of support for the regime, fundamental economic reform is impossible.

Thirdly, some analysts suggest that the United States can avoid paying the price of confronting friendly Arab regimes with demands for democratic reform by instead cultivating indigenous civil-society activists, who can raise their own internal demands for change. Arab civil society, some suggest, can produce velvet revolutions in Damascus and Cairo just as Eastern European dissidents did in Prague and Budapest.

But Western civil-society assistance, unaccompanied by high-level diplomatic dialogue to support internal reformists, is unlikely to have much effect. Most Arab states severely restrict freedom of association, making it very difficult for liberal activists to meet and organize, much less demonstrate for change. And there is no framework like the Helsinki Agreement to provide cover for such activists to challenge these internal constraints.[5] As a result, Arab civil society is weak and constantly under threat (and, as noted above, secular reformers are severely disadvantaged relative to Islamist groups). Without external pressure on regimes to allow political organization to proceed, civil society has little hope of challenging the balance of power inside any single Arab state.

Finally, those who suggest that America support gradual, limited liberalization, embrace economic growth as a long-term path to democracy, or restrict ourselves to bottom-up approaches neglect the urgency of the challenge we face in the Arab Middle East. The stagnation and passivity that characterize Arab society and politics create sympathetic support for Binladenism *today*, and a strategy to combat those problems that relies on a decade or more of economic

---

3 For a complete discussion of Tunisia's failed reform, see Eva Bellin, *Stalled Democracy: Capital, Labor, and the Paradox of State-Sponsored Development* (Ithaca, NY: Cornell University Press, 2002).

4 For more on the failed links between economic and political reform in the region, see Tarik M. Yousef, "Development, Growth, and Policy Reform in the Middle East and North Africa Since 1950," *Journal of Economic Perspectives* 18, no.3 (Summer 2004): 91–116.

5 The Broader Middle East Initiative (BMENA), though conceived with the Helsinki Accords in mind, does not provide the fundamental quid pro quo that Helsinki contained, of sovereignty protections in exchange for human rights progress. Moreover, it does not bind the Arab states as signatories but treats them as targets or subjects of the initiative.

growth as a trigger for further change, or a generational shift in educational curricula, consigns us to at least another twenty years of an expanding circle of bin Laden supporters. Such a strategy is simply insufficient to address our needs. The United States can and must promote changes in Arab politics and society that allow voices to arise that will directly confront Binladenism with progressive alternatives to its cult of death—an ideology that can only be attractive to a wide audience in the perceived absence of other options.

An effective pro-reform policy must therefore be comprehensive—one that does not privilege economic over political reform and that does not ignore urgent problems for the sake of long-term social reform. Our policy must combine incentives for regimes to change their top-down policies with assistance for civil society to meet those policy changes with bottom-up demand for further reforms.

Setting Reform Priorities

With this background in mind, American priorities in promoting Middle Eastern reform in the coming four years become clearer. America cannot restrict its pro-reform efforts to one dimension of change, since economic, political, and social reform are intimately related in the realities of today's Arab world. But in embracing a comprehensive vision of regional reform, the United States can and should distinguish between more urgent goals and those that can only be achieved more gradually. One can also set reform priorities with an eye to reducing the risks of a pro-reform policy to other U.S. interests.

Our goals for the period 2005–2009 should be:

1. *Economic Liberalization:*
   a. In the **short term,** to absorb young entrants to the labor market, to provide younger generations the possibility of improving their socioeconomic prospects, and to improve the transparency and accountability of government spending;
   b. In the **longer term,** to improve the distribution of wealth across societies, to dismantle the economic structures that sustain corrupt and authoritarian regimes, and to facilitate broader participation in the global economy.

2. *Educational Reforms:*
   a. In the **short term,** to help young people gain employable skills and to reduce the employment of prejudiced or inflammatory material (or instructors) in the curriculum;
   b. In the **longer term,** to teach younger generations to think critically so as to reduce the appeal of extremist ideology, and to enhance civic education to build an active and engaged citizenry committed to toleration and to the practice of democracy.

3. *Political liberalization*
   a. In the **short term,** to increase government responsiveness, transparency, and accountability to citizens so as to reduce alienation and resentment; and to create the conditions (including improved rights to free association and free press) necessary for the emergence of liberal and other political movements so as to undermine Islamist advantages in political discourse and build the foundations for democratic politics;
   b. In the **longer term,** to promote reforms of constitutions, political institutions, the judiciary, and the police and security services in the direction of liberal democracy (including political rights), and to press for the holding of open, competitive elections for parliamentary and executive authorities— all in order to build more legitimate and more stable Arab regimes and to promote moderate politics.

WHERE SHOULD WE FOCUS OUR EFFORTS?

In pursuing these goals, the United States must also consider *where* in the Arab world to concentrate our efforts. Over the past four years, the trend has been toward regionally addressed programs, such as the Middle East Partnership Initiative and the Broader Middle East Initiative (BMENA). The rationale for a broad, cross-regional approach has been to create demonstration projects in different issue-areas and to create a competitive dynamic between reform-minded Arab leaders, with each vying for our recognition and rewards in the form of assistance and trade ties. This approach has yielded uneven results, since it relies ultimately on the interest of regional leaders in embracing reform, regardless of the importance of the country involved to the regional picture or to U.S. interests. These efforts have also been constrained by the very limited resources they have had to work with.

The 21 Arab states and the Palestinian territories are very differently situated with respect to political, economic, and social reform. Some Arab leaders have already undertaken fundamental decisions to reform economic structures (Jordan, United Arab Emirates), education (Qatar) or the distribution of political power (Yemen). Many others remain caught between the risks of reform and the pain of continued stagnation. For those regimes already prepared to take risks for certain reforms (notably the Jordanian and Moroccan monarchs), the recognition and limited benefits the U.S. government has put on offer have been effective incentives—but the competitive dynamic has sometimes backfired, leading some leaders to give up momentum in their domestic reforms (Syria). In other cases, the region-wide approach laid out by the U.S. government has been set aside in favor of assistance to Arab regimes of special interest to the United States (Egypt is most notable in this regard).

The United States also has more developed, multifaceted, and interdependent relations with some Arab states than with others, and these relations provide leverage even as they increase our risk profile in promoting change. Whether and how to link the imperative of reform to other aspects of our bilateral relations with key Arab states like Egypt or Saudi Arabia is a central challenge in constructing a viable and effective pro-reform strategy.

Finally, some Arab states' fates will weigh more heavily on the region's future than others. While the small Gulf emirates may make swift progress in implementing economic and educational reforms, their small size and geographical isolation means that their societies' progress and prospects will have only a marginal effect on their larger Arab neighbors. But the future of Egypt, with 70 million people, Iraq, with 25 million, and Algeria, with 30 million, will have a decided impact not only on the Middle East's overall developmental health, but on the progress of economic globalization. And in the same fashion, the failure of even a single major Arab state to overcome its demographic challenge could result in a destabilization of the region. Imagine, for example, the effect of wide-scale social instability in Egypt or Saudi Arabia on American interests in regional security and stable energy production.

In the coming term, the U.S. government should focus its efforts on key Arab states with whom we have multifaceted relationships and thus significant leverage over and interest in their domestic reform process. Our efforts should be focused on helping cultivate the political will and leadership in those countries that is necessary to decide upon and implement important structural reforms in politics and economics. In some cases, carefully structured incentives provided by the United States might make a decisive difference in the attitudes of political leaders toward reform.

Such bilateral efforts should be complemented by continued engagement with regional states in multilateral groupings such as BMENA's "Forum for the Future"—but the main goal of the multilateral sessions should be to use the Forum's high profile and inclusion of non-governmental stakeholders to consolidate and build momentum for bilateral efforts and individual initiatives, rather than to pursue cross-regional projects whose impact on any local governance situation is likely to be limited and gradual.

One can establish a three-tiered ranking of major Arab states based on the above discussion. This framework is not comprehensive, but provides guidance in setting priorities for American policy:

- **Egypt** and **Saudi Arabia** stand out for both the depth of their relationship with the United States and for the importance of their domestic stability and evolution on broader regional developments. Indeed, 2005 is a critical year for Egyptian political reform, with President Mubarak planning to enter an unprecedented fifth term in an uncontested national referendum, and with parliamentary elections scheduled for the fall. America's attitude toward these moves by our closest Arab ally will greatly determine our credibility and impact on political reform regionwide.[6]

- **Morocco, Algeria, and Yemen** represent Arab states with sizeable populations and a noticeable ability to impact regional prospects, and with whom the United States has sufficient interaction to help shape developments. **Syria** has a troubled relationship with the United States, but its role in the Arab-Israeli conflict, its domination of Lebanese politics, and its shared border with Iraq enhances the importance of our interactions and gives us an additional stake in Syria's future as well as additional leverage over its regime.

- **Jordan, Qatar, Tunisia, Bahrain, and Kuwait** represent a third tier of states whose economic and demographic weight in the region may be of less significance, but whose political leaders and relationship with the United States may prove influential. Pro-reform developments in these states may serve to enhance the momentum of change by providing a demonstration effect, but the tangible effects of developments in these states on other Arab countries are likely to be limited.

ELEMENTS OF AN EFFECTIVE PRO-REFORM POLICY

All elements of America's foreign policy arsenal must be marshaled on behalf of an effective pro-reform policy in the Arab Middle East. Some elements of our current relationships with Arab governments will require restructuring, while others must be carefully preserved.

BILATERAL DIPLOMACY

American foreign policy must clearly communicate to Arab governments—publicly and privately, and at senior levels—that states that are actually changing the distribution of political power will enjoy better relations with the United States than

---

6 A detailed country strategy for Egypt in 2005 is beyond the scope of this paper. Nonetheless, while the United States may determine that policy considerations militate against pressing for competitive Egyptian presidential elections this year, the U.S. government should press hard to ensure that applications for new political parties are approved, that open and critical media coverage of the campaign is encouraged, that constitutional mechanisms are fully adhered to, that judicial oversight of the election is comprehensive, independent, and unchallenged, that citizen monitoring and engagement are fully enabled, and that no voting irregularities are allowed. More broadly, the United States can communicate to President Mubarak that his fifth unchallenged term in office must be his last, and should be devoted to preparing the ground for a transition to an open and competitive political system—in other words, that this year's elections should be viewed as the last of their kind in Egypt. For another discussion of American strategy toward Egypt, see Michele Durocher Dunne, "Integrating Democracy Promotion into U.S. Middle East Policy," Carnegie Endowment for International Peace Working Paper #50 (Washington: Carnegie Endowment, October 2004).

those that talk about reform but fail to implement it. U.S. government representatives must communicate clear and specific expectations of reform in a given partner nation consistently at every level of dialogue. Transparency in our communications about reform enhances our effectiveness by giving local reform activists cover for their own efforts. Simultaneously, transparency helps protect the United States from accusations of hidden agendas or secret deals with dictators. The symbolic aspects of our bilateral relations: state and ministerial exchanges of visits, non-NATO partner status, port visits, and the like can all be used to emphasize close ties to reforming regimes and can be held out as incentives for reluctant reformers. Under certain circumstances, public expressions of bilateral relations can be adjusted downward as well to increase pressure on recalcitrant Arab leaders.[7]

In raising the profile of democratic reform in our bilateral relations with Arab states, the United States can take note of where shared interests with its Arab interlocutors will help mediate the tensions that an effective democratization effort is bound to create. America's relations with key states in the region are grounded in a web of longstanding mutual interests and benefits. Such relationships can withstand a greater degree of tension than they have generally witnessed—as indeed has been demonstrated repeatedly in the three years since 9/11. Riyadh and Washington share interests in the strategic defense of the Gulf and stability in the price of oil, and they still would, even if the United States were to push Saudi Arabia harder on political reform. Egypt today pursues Palestinian-Israeli rapprochement for its own reasons—sometimes with greater initiative than the United States itself. There is no reason to expect that the Mubarak regime would sacrifice its self-interested engagement in promoting an Israeli-Palestinian peace settlement simply in order to express its displeasure with American pressure for political reform. Indeed, the developments of the past year suggest the reverse may be true, and that Egypt's government might accelerate its cooperation on the peace process in an attempt to deflect American pressure for internal reform.

ASSISTANCE

The question of conditioning U.S. bilateral aid to Arab governments on their commitment to democratic reform is perhaps the most controversial issue in building a pro-reform policy. On the one hand, existing aid programs designed to encourage gradual reform through entirely consensual projects have a very limited record of success, suggesting that "tougher" measures are appropriate. On the other hand, altering the composition and conditions of longstanding U.S. aid programs in countries such as Egypt is likely to induce a backlash perhaps more quickly than any other American policy shift.

Some simply reject the idea of conditionality as inconsistent with the principle of "partnership" with the Arab world. If by partnership we mean partnering with Arab governments, then that may be true. But if by partnership we mean partnering with Arab citizens who want to improve their lives and who individually are the ones who choose to stay at home or to migrate, to remain productive citizens or to join a violent radical movement, then conditioning our relations with Arab governments on their behavior toward their citizens seems wholly appropriate. While maintaining working relations with Arab leaders, the United States must never fail to emphasize its alliance with Arab citizens in their struggle for a better future.

---

7 This, too can be symbolic—as was the case in 2003, when President Bush announced that, because of Egypt's continued persecution of dual U.S. citizen Saad Eddin Ibrahim, he could not bring before Congress any supplemental aid request to Egypt; no such aid request had been made at the time, but the message to Cairo was unequivocal and effective.

Rather than reducing extant aid amounts or placing new conditions on long-standing aid, the United States should in most cases focus on building strict conditionality into all *new* bilateral assistance proposals. One lever already available is that several Arab governments are interested in qualifying for Millennium Challenge Account funds, eligibility for which includes governance criteria. In countries like Morocco, where the Administration plans to increase development assistance, we should ensure that AID-Morocco's future is clearly tied to its independence of action in funding democracy and governance programs.

Conditionality should extend beyond assistance, in fact, to include all potential enhancements in bilateral relations, such as trade agreements, high-level visits, and other benefits. Carefully structured bilateral packages can provide incentives for desired change to overcome the specific concerns of recalcitrant governments. For example, if security-sector reform threatens the economic well-being of a country's officer corps, specific assistance to provide job retraining, private-sector investment credits, or even pensions might be made available in exchange for specific action by the recipient government. Egypt, America's largest Arab aid recipient excluding Iraq, agreed in 1998 to a 10-percent per-year reduction in assistance, despite the country's continued need for development aid.[8] The "lost" assistance, which took the form of cash transfers and commodity import credits, could be replaced by new, conditional, carefully targeted assistance to encourage or reinforce desired reforms.

At the same time, the United States should use region-wide programs to build new relationships centered around reform with Arab government agencies, the private sector, and nongovernmental groups. Regional programs will attract those governments who are already committed to pro-reform policies, providing a reward for good policy choices as well as a demonstration effect for other countries in the region.

The most efficient and transparent means for doing this would be a new U.S.-Arab Democracy Challenge Account. This would be modeled in part on the Millennium Challenge Account, another program that was explicitly designed to change the incentive structure for governments in making development-related policies—but it would be more multifaceted in implementation. The *Democracy Challenge Account* would include government-to-government assistance for countries that meet certain governance-related criteria and that clearly demonstrate their commitment to democratization and the rule of law. It would also include civil-society assistance programs that would be undertaken independently from regular bilateral assistance—like the Middle East Partnership Initiative—but that would be tied explicitly to democratic reform efforts at the societal level, including political party development, advocacy, civic education, and the like. Finally, the Democracy Challenge Account should include incentives (for example, loan or investment guarantees, tax incentives, or favorable credit) for American businesses to expand their relations with Arab counterparts in countries that are committed to real economic *and* political reform. This private-sector component could be similar to the incentives provided by the U.S. government to U.S. businesses to invest in Israel in support of the Middle East peace process in the early 1990s.

Reform-focused assistance should not neglect the military and security services of Arab countries, but the United States must avoid the temptation to quickly condition all its existing military assistance to Arab states on political

---

8 This reduction was negotiated to accord with a simultaneous reduction in U.S. assistance to Israel, despite the widely disparate economic situations in the two countries.

reform. By and large, America's military assistance programs in the Arab world help to secure high-value cooperation with American strategic goals, while preserving local militaries' reliance on U.S. equipment, spare parts, and training. In addition, ongoing cooperation with and training of Arab military officers helps promote the professionalization and independence from politics of Arab military institutions—and this in turn produces a more favorable climate for democratic development in an area of the world where military meddling in business and politics has been long-standing.[9] That said, conditioning military aid might be effective in certain circumstances, for example where there is evidence of human rights abuses by recipient agencies or direct interference by the military in political affairs, or where such aid serves to solidify the military's support for autocracy rather than move it away from political involvement.

TRANSATLANTIC COOPERATION

While disagreements over methodology remain relevant, both the United States and the European powers now agree on the desirability, for self-interested as well as for altruistic reasons, of democratic reform in the Arab world. This shared declaration of intent was the most important outcome of last year's G-8 initiative on the Broader Middle East.[10]

In its transatlantic diplomacy on this issue, the United States should continue to emphasize the shared goals of democracy, human rights promotion, and political moderation along with the oft-cited goals of economic prosperity and integration of the Arab world into the global trading system. America and European countries may pursue these goals largely separately, but mechanisms for coordination through the G-8 should be encouraged and maintained.

Foremost among these is the Democracy Assistance Dialogue (DAD) created in the Broader Middle East Initiative. The DAD is chaired jointly by Italy, Turkey, and Yemen, and is meant to coordinate between governments providing democracy assistance, implementing agencies like the various party foundations in the United States and Germany, and local Arab NGOs who receive funds and participate in programs. Through its G-8 sponsorship, the DAD should become a means whereby local Arab activists can highlight arenas ripe for democratic development in their countries to which Western assistance can be directed, and whereby action items for higher-level government policy can be formulated and channeled to the G-8 governments for action. Thus, for example, media training by U.S.-based NGOs can be coordinated with European funding for exchange visits, and local journalists pushing the boundaries of press freedom in their societies can highlight official obstacles they face as issues to be raised by Western governments in diplomatic meetings.

HEDGING AGAINST RISK

For purposes of cultivating alternative opposition movements to radical Islamists, and thus minimizing the risks that Islamists will take advantage of political openings to the detriment of U.S. interests, the most important reforms the Administration can push for are those that will both strengthen liberal political movements and strengthen the ability of Arab societies to debate, test, and hopefully reject the claims of radical Islamist movements. The United States must press Arab leaders for top-down reforms in order to level the playing field that is currently tilted against liberal Arab voices. These reforms are, not coincidentally, also the ones most likely to be resisted by governments as undermining their

---

9 See Mehran Kamrava, "Military Professionalization and Civil-Military Relations in the Middle East," *Political Science Quarterly* 115, no. 1 (Spring 2000): 67–93.

10 For further discussion of transatlantic cooperation on Arab-world democracy promotion, see Tamara Cofman Wittes, "Promoting Democracy in the Arab World: The Challenge of Joint Action," *The International Spectator* 34:4 (December 2004): 75–88.

authority: the legalization of alternative political parties, establishing or expanding the freedom of associational life, cultivating a freer broadcast and print media, and increasing the diversity of content on national broadcast media. The United States can also subsidize the propagation of alternative voices by supporting liberal groups, encouraging the study of liberal ideas from within the Muslim world's rich intellectual tradition, and funding the translation and dissemination of key works of Western liberal political philosophy into Arabic.

In addition, there are simultaneous steps the U.S. government can take to hedge against the possibility that Islamist parties might in fact triumph in a competitive political process in some Arab countries. These steps include establishing and maintaining dialogue with those Islamist leaders and movements who commit to fundamental rules of liberal democracy—limited government with accountability through legislative oversight, courts, and the electoral process, individual rights guaranteed through rule of law, rejection and delegitimation of violence, and other extralegal means of influencing politics. There is a perception in the region today that the United States is blacklisting Islamist groups or movements, or is not interested in including them in its assistance programs. That's a dangerous impression, and worse if true. Dialogue does not imply irrevocable recognition, a fact that was demonstrated by the U.S. dialogues with the PLO in 1988 and the Taliban (over the disposition of Usama bin Laden) ten years later. In opening such a dialogue, the Bush Administration can build on its experience working with Islamist movements within Iraq to generate lessons and guidelines for engagement elsewhere.

The United States can also work in its communications with opposition groups and in its training activities for political activists to encourage dialogue between Islamist and non-Islamist pro-democracy opposition movements. To the extent that such groups can agree on goals or rules for a transition to democracy, they can present a powerful set of demands to the existing leadership.

America's attitude toward Islamist opposition movements should be varied, according to the movements' characteristics and according to the policies of the regime under which they are operating. An Islamist movement's commitment to the democratic process cannot be tested until there is a process in which they can choose to engage. If an Arab government is taking meaningful steps to facilitate associational life and cultivate broader debate, and some movements take advantage of that greater openness to advance violence or other anti-democratic means of influencing politics, then the United States should be willing to tolerate the regime's repression of those forces. But we should not accede to those regimes that would use the excuse of radical Islamist activity to crack down on all Islamist groups. In Jordan, after some years of Islamist participation in parliament, the Islamist parties that participate in politics have begun to fracture, with more ideological members abandoning electoral politics, and with the Islamists in parliament as a result becoming more uniformly "moderate." Over time, a legitimate and meaningful political process will marginalize those remaining ideological extremists. But if over time the parliamentary system is perceived instead as window dressing on an absolute monarchy, then it is the moderate Islamists who will be discredited, while the radicals will grow in popularity. Cultivating a moderate Islamist movement will be an important part of successful democratization in many Arab societies—but the legitimacy of a moderate Islamist political discourse will hinge on the legitimacy of the democratization process overall.

Practically speaking, there are also steps that the United States can take to reduce the risk that a more assertive pro-reform policy will undermine U.S.-Arab cooperation on other issues. Wherever possible, the United States should work to anchor relevant Arab government policy in international commitments—multilateral or to an international governmental organization—rather than simply to the bilateral relationship. In the worst case, should an existing government fall to radical nationalist or Islamist forces, those policies that are most directly tied to a bilateral relationship with the United States are most likely to be targeted for revision, whereas international obligations will retain a claim. Instruments to enable this sort of hedge might include:

- Multilateral agreements on corruption, terrorist financing, and human rights;

- International trading regimes that include strong transparency and rule-of-law mechanisms;

- Maritime treaties (such as the Law of the Sea Treaty) for freedom of access/navigation;

- Multilateral agreements and programs to promote reform, including BMENA instruments and ad hoc transatlantic cooperative projects that condition valuable goods on Arab government policies.

CONCLUSION: DEMOCRATIZATION, CREDIBILITY AND PUBLIC DIPLOMACY

Critics of a pro-reform policy often note America's weak credibility with Arab elites and publics, citing our unpopular policies in Iraq and the Israeli-Palestinian arena and our past history of supporting autocratic regimes. In the face of such obstacles, they suggest, America's attempts to promote regional reform will inevitably be negatively perceived by the Arab public, and thus cannot be effective.

In the final analysis, American credibility with the Arab public in speaking about democratic development will be a function of the substance of our pro-democracy policy. If we demonstrate a willingness to pursue our interest in democratic reform alongside, and sometimes at the risk of, our other interests in the region, then our words will acquire credibility. If we continue to align our preferences with those of regional leaders for incremental, limited liberalization that has little political content, our policy will continue to lack credibility with recalcitrant autocrats, with aspiring liberal activists, or with the grassroots they one day hope to enlist in their cause.

Policy credibility, however, is a distinct issue from the popularity of American policy or of America itself in the region. A pro-reform policy cannot properly be viewed as part of a public diplomacy strategy to enhance American popularity in the Middle East. This is evident in that an effective pro-reform policy requires empowering diverse political elements who may or may not agree with U.S. policy preferences. And it is quite possible, even likely, that more democratic Arab regimes would reflect in their own public diplomacy the popular resentment of American policies in Iraq and Israel.

Deeper and more meaningful than any attempt to "win hearts and minds" for America itself, the forward strategy of freedom should be understood as an effort to win Arab hearts and minds over to the practice of liberal values and virtues —whether the new practitioners ultimately embrace America and its policies or not. In so doing, the forward strategy must be integrated with our other policy goals, but cannot abandon the imperatives of promoting regional stability and undermining extremism.

Achieving Middle East Peace

Martin Indyk

Any discussion of what to do about the new sense of opportunity in Israeli-Palestinian relations has to start from acknowledging two contradictory realities. On the negative side of the ledger, the conflict between Israel and the Palestinians that has raged for the last four years, claiming over 3,000 Palestinian and 1,000 Israeli lives, has destroyed the Oslo process, much of the Palestinian Authority created by it, and the rest of the edifice of Israeli-Palestinian peacemaking that the United States helped so painstakingly to build over the previous twelve years. Consequently, the Palestinian leadership that is now emerging in the wake of Arafat's death lacks the basic infrastructure of government to exercise its responsibilities effectively in any renewed peacemaking effort. Meanwhile, Israelis have become so disillusioned with the idea of reconciliation with the Palestinians that they prefer unilateral steps to the normal approach of making peace between two parties based on mutual respect and recognition.

Coexisting uneasily with this dismal reality, however, is a widespread consensus in support of a final settlement based on the creation of a Palestinian state in the West Bank and Gaza living alongside a secure, Jewish state of Israel.

This consensus encompasses a clear majority of Israelis and Palestinians, most Arab leaders if not yet their people, much of the international community, and most Americans (including a majority within the American Jewish community). As Shimon Peres has observed, "There is a light at the end of the tunnel; there's just no tunnel."

The challenge for the Bush Administration, in its second term, will be to reconcile these two seemingly contradictory realities. In theory, the strategy is obvious: use the consensus about the end result to shine light into the tunnel, while systematically working with the new Palestinian leadership, Israel, Arab states and the Quartet (the European Union, Russia and the United Nations) to rebuild the tunnel itself. To turn that theory into a new reality, however, will require sustained Presidential engagement with all of the players, a commitment of substantial American resources, a willingness to bear political costs, and, above all, a strategy that generates a positive regional balance of power. This last role is arguably the most valuable contribution the United States can make to Middle East peacemaking and the one it is most capable of making.

MAINTAINING THE BALANCE

As pointed out in the Introduction, the Bush Administration, in its second term, needs to develop a more integrated strategy for the Middle East. In such an integrated approach, progress on one policy track would reinforce progress on others and help to buttress the overall strategy from the inevitable setbacks that can and will occur on individual tracks. Stabilizing Iraq, for example, would enable the devotion of more attention and resources to Middle East peacemaking; incorporating Syria into a peacemaking strategy could help reinforce its cooperation over Iraq; deterring Iranian support for Palestinian terrorism would make it easier to achieve an Israeli-Palestinian ceasefire, etc.

The need for this kind of symbiosis in policy is especially acute with regard to Arab-Israeli peacemaking. In particular, progress on all tracks of an integrated strategy for the Middle East would help create a favorable regional balance of power in which moderate forces would be strengthened and Islamic extremist forces would find themselves increasingly on the defensive. Altering these region-wide realities of power will in turn impact on the local realities that currently make any peacemaking effort look foolish. For example, reengaging Syria and the Arab states in the peacemaking efforts could engender hope for reconciliation in the minds of Israelis who have been persuaded by Palestinian terrorism and Arab support for it that there is no Arab partner for peace. Similarly, cutting Iranian and Syrian support for Palestinian terror would make it easier to achieve the elusive Palestinian ceasefire that is the precondition to any progress on the political level.

Nevertheless, pursuing policies that will have a positive impact on the regional balance of power and, therefore, the external environment for peacemaking will fall short of the desired impact if they are not accompanied by two parallel, internal efforts:

- to strengthen the ability of the Palestinian Authority and the government of Israel to engage in the effort of achieving an historic reconciliation (i.e. "rebuilding the tunnel"), and

- to provide both sides with incentives to overcome the extremists within their midst (i.e. "shining light into the tunnel").

REBUILDING THE TUNNEL

Arafat's demise has created a significant opening for a new, more responsible, reform-minded Palestinian leadership to emerge under Abu Mazen (Mahmoud Abbas). The Bush Administration's objective should be to exploit this opportunity to encourage and support Abu Mazen and an elected Palestinian Authority in becoming credible, capable, and legitimate partners for peacemaking.

There is considerable urgency to this delicate process. Abu Mazen was elected president of the Palestinian Authority with a highly respectable 62 percent of the vote, which gives him a clear mandate to end the terrorism of the *intifada* and resume the effort to secure Palestinian rights through negotiations rather than violence. But his popular mandate will soon evaporate if he is unable to prove to his people that he can deliver in a way that Arafat could not—by improving their daily lives and reducing, and eventually ending, the occupation.

In 2002, a similar opportunity arose, when Palestinians forced Arafat to appoint Abu Mazen prime minister and he promptly negotiated a *hudna* (ceasefire) with Hamas. But the Bush Administration and the Sharon Government were too skeptical to lend him a serious hand and Arafat exploited their hesitation to undermine Abu Mazen, forcing his resignation after only three months in office. The United States and Israel need to learn the lesson of that experience and not miss a moment of opportunity again.

The first place where Abu Mazen can be seen to be delivering is in Gaza where, as the Israeli disengagement goes forward, coordination with them could help to ensure that the Palestinian Authority fills the vacuum left by Israel's withdrawal. As long as Arafat was in control, Sharon refused to countenance coordination, but he now has an interest in showing Israelis that responsible Palestinian leadership is taking over in Gaza as a result of his initiative.

The first, tentative steps in this regard already reveal the potential for coordination in Gaza to rebuild confidence on both sides. Abu Mazen has negotiated a new hudna with Hamas and the other militant organizations and has deployed thousands of police officers in northern Gaza to prevent Kassam rocket attacks on southern Israel. Sharon has reciprocated by staying the IDF's hand and easing restrictions on the movement of Gazans. But the process is vulnerable to the next terror attack, and the militants, backed by Hizballah and Iran, have a deep interest in demonstrating that their use of violence rather than Abu Mazen's restoration of order is responsible for the departure of the Israeli soldiers and settlers from Gaza.

Moreover, West Bank Palestinians will be wary of this "Gaza first" process because of their fear that it will be "Gaza last" and their interests will be ignored. Sharon will need to be encouraged to take actions in the West Bank too, in coordination with Abu Mazen, to dismantle settlement outposts (something he repeatedly promised President Bush he would do), remove unnecessary roadblocks and release significant numbers of prisoners.[1] West Bankers will be particularly keen to see the resumption of negotiations over the fate of their territory; something Sharon will be reluctant to do because of his concern that this will inevitably generate pressure on Israel to give

up most of the West Bank. In the wake of Arafat's departure, Sharon has already emphasized the need to return to the Roadmap, which requires Palestinians to dismantle the terrorist infrastructure before negotiations on the disposition of West Bank territory begin.

This is a reasonable requirement given the role that terror has played in destroying the peace process as well as the lives of innocents. However, with Arafat's obstructionist capabilities reduced if not eliminated, it should be more possible to build a new Palestinian security capacity to disarm the terrorists. And, if the end game is spelled out in more detail (see below), it should also be possible to give the new Palestinian leadership additional credible reasons for acting against the terrorists once the memory of Abu Mazen's popular mandate begins to fade.

The most effective way to legitimize and empower a new Palestinian leadership, however, would be through the holding of legislative elections in both Gaza and the West Bank. Arafat had opposed the call from Palestinians for new elections precisely because he understood that it would legitimize new leaders. But the Palestinian Authority has now announced the holding of elections for the Legislative Council in July 2005. They would need to take place under the new constitution, which has already been drafted, which would invest power in a prime minister and cabinet responsible to the newly-elected Legislative Council. Legislative Council elections would provide an opportunity to young guard Palestinian nationalists and reformers to assume positions of responsibility in the Palestinian Authority. It would also give Hamas, which has declared its intention of running candidates, the opportunity to enter mainstream Palestinian politics, provided it was made clear to them that they

---

1 Israel is reported to be detaining over 10,000 Palestinians, only some 1,000 of whom are accused of having blood on their hands.

would have to give up their arms as the precondition to their participation.

REBUILDING PALESTINIAN CAPACITY:

Even if Arafat's departure and elections enable the emergence of a new, more responsible and accountable Palestinian leadership, it will still face the serious problem of a lack of capacity to fulfill any commitments it might enter into to end the violence and dismantle the terror infrastructure. To rebuild this Palestinian capacity, the United States would have to initiate a serious and sustained international effort to build the institutions of a democratic Palestinian state from the ground up: representative and accountable political institutions, transparent economic institutions, an independent judiciary, and a restructured and retrained security apparatus.

Some aspects of this effort are already under way (e.g. the Palestinian finance minister has made significant progress in reforming the way the Palestinian Authority does business). But Arafat persistently stymied other efforts, particularly on the security front. His death will open the way to these essential reforms, but they will not happen without an active, sustained, American-led, international effort to help uncorrupted, reform-minded Palestinians rebuild these institutions.

On the Israeli side, the single most important factor that will help create an environment for reinvigorated peacemaking is an end to Palestinian violence and terror. If this is the product of a Palestinian reform process that removes Arafat's negative legacy and restores order to Gaza, it will do much to re-engender Israelis' faith in the idea that they have a peacemaking partner.

THE GAZA DISENGAGEMENT SPRINGBOARD:

The implementation of Prime Minister Sharon's disengagement plan, expected to be completed by October 2005, will also dramatically impact Israeli attitudes toward peacemaking. Assuming it takes place as planned, the evacuation of all Israeli settlers from the Gaza Strip will establish an important precedent for similar steps on the West Bank. It will manifest the will of an Israeli majority over a determined minority of the settlers and their supporters in the nationalist bloc. It might also consolidate the broad-based coalition government that Sharon has now formed with the Labor Party and segments of the religious bloc, making it possible for him to proceed into negotiations over the West Bank and Jerusalem once the Gaza disengagement is completed.

Sharon himself will be reluctant to move beyond the Gaza disengagement because he hopes to retain as much high ground in the West Bank as possible until the Palestinians undergo a fundamental transformation in their attitudes toward Israel. If chaos and anarchy fill the vacuum left by Israel's withdrawal from Gaza and rocket attacks on Israeli towns continue, the clear absence of a Palestinian partner will reinforce Israeli skepticism and provide political backing for Sharon's strategy of a long-term interim solution that leaves Israel in control of some 50 percent of the West Bank. The prevailing view may well be that Israel cannot risk a similar failed terror state on the West Bank by withdrawing from there.

Accordingly, Israel's disengagement from Gaza provides an opportunity and a danger for U.S. policy. The opportunity lies in Israel's complete withdrawal, which creates the circumstances for Palestinians to rule themselves in Gaza without Israeli interference or control.

If a new Palestinian leadership were to begin to exercise responsibility in Gaza, it could provide an example to Israelis and Palestinians alike of the benefits of ending occupation. If, however, the withdrawal is followed by chaos, anarchy and more attacks on Israel, it will provide further proof to Israelis that they have no partner.

Before Arafat's death, all the vectors were pointing in the direction of a Gaza disaster. Egyptian efforts to restructure and retrain the security services and negotiate a ceasefire agreement between the various factions had stalled. World Bank plans for rebuilding the Gaza economy remained on paper, awaiting a calmer environment for implementation. Potential international donors were reluctant to pledge significant financial support because they experienced how the billions of dollars they had invested in building the Gaza infrastructure were wasted in the destruction wrought by the intifada.

As already suggested, Arafat's passing creates an opportunity for coordinating Israel's disengagement with the new Palestinian leadership. And that could facilitate the additional steps necessary to turn the Gaza disengagement into a springboard for progress on peacemaking:

- The administration would first need to get behind Abu Mazen's efforts to negotiate a lasting ceasefire among the Palestinian factions (with tacit cooperation from Israel).

- The Gaza security forces would need to be restructured and retrained.

- The United States and Egypt would need to make effective security arrangements to prevent smuggling of arms into Gaza, which would enable Israel to make a complete withdrawal, including from the Philadelphi Corridor (between Gaza and Egypt), the passages, and Gaza's sea and air space.

- The United States would also need to partner with the World Bank in an active effort to generate international support for the rebuilding of the Gaza economy and the provision of quick-start employment projects.

SHINING LIGHT INTO THE TUNNEL

Such efforts to make the Israeli disengagement from Gaza and the empowerment of a new Palestinian leadership the first steps in a renewed peacemaking strategy are more likely to succeed if they are accompanied by a parallel effort to give Israelis and Palestinians a clearer sense of where the process is going. At the moment, the open-ended nature of the putative "Roadmap" process does nothing to rebuild confidence: Palestinians are promised a viable state but see Israeli settlement expansion making that impossible; Israelis are promised security but experience only terrorism and violence. Both sides need to believe again that an eventual peaceful resolution of their conflict is possible.

That can come from Palestinian efforts to stop the violence and Israeli efforts to freeze West Bank settlement activity, as called for in Phase I of the Roadmap. But such confidence building measures require leaders on both sides to confront militant constituencies of Islamic extremists and nationalist settlers. To do so, they will need the backing of moderate majorities that the bloody conflict of the last four years has immobilized.

An important way of mobilizing those majorities is for President Bush to portray and incorporate into the Roadmap a more detailed picture of the end game the United States and the international community, including the Arab world, would support. The timing of such a statement would be important. It could be done in stages, starting with a letter of assurance to Palestinian President Mahmoud Abbas to complement the letter President Bush gave to Prime Minister Sharon in 2004. It could be outlined in a Presidential address after the Gaza disengagement is completed in the fall of 2005. Or it could be presented to the International Conference that is called for in Phase II of the Roadmap.

The outlines of a final Israeli-Palestinian settlement are no mystery, as they have been subjected to detailed negotiations in the last year of the Clinton Administration and detailed discussion ever since. They would have to be based more or less on the following principles:

1. Two states for two people: a viable, democratic state of Palestine, living in peace alongside a secure, Jewish, democratic state of Israel.

2. The Palestinian state to be established on 95–97 percent of the West Bank and all of the Gaza Strip, with territorial compensation for the 3–5 percent of the West Bank foregone.

3. Israeli settlers on the West Bank to be concentrated in three settlement blocs adjacent to the 1967 lines on territory annexed to Israel (not to exceed 5 percent of the West Bank).

4. Palestinian refugees to have the right of return to the state of Palestine but not to Israel, with appropriate compensation and the option of resettlement in third countries.

5. Jerusalem to serve as one capital for the two states, a united city in which what is Arab in east Jerusalem will come under Palestinian sovereignty and what is Jewish will come under Israeli sovereignty.[2]

6. Security arrangements, including the demilitarization of the Palestinian state, to reconcile the right of Israel to defend itself and protect its citizens with the right of Palestine to a viable, contiguous state in the West Bank, linked to Gaza.

7. An end to the Arab-Israeli conflict and recognition of Israel by all Arab states.

If President Bush were to articulate these principles and they were immediately endorsed by Arab leaders, Israelis and Palestinians would then have a much better sense of the final destination before they were asked again to embark on the path of a negotiated settlement. They would see not only what they were expected to give up but also what they would get in return when the final deal was eventually struck.[3]

- For example, Israelis would know that if they were prepared to relinquish their hold on the West Bank, the Palestinians would have to give up their demand for the right of return to Israel—i.e. the demographic threat to the Jewish state would be terminated.

- Palestinians would know that if they relinquished violence and terror in favor of negotiations they would achieve their legitimate aspirations for a viable, contiguous state in the West Bank and Gaza—i.e. most West Bank settlements would be evacuated. Israelis would also know that the wider Arab-Israeli conflict would be ended, replaced by recognition and normalization of relations with the Arab world. Palestinians would also know that they would be adequately reimbursed with territory and financial compensation for compromises that allowed for Israel's annexation of settlement blocs along the 1967 lines and the foregoing of the "right of return."

---

2 The status in a final settlement of the Jewish, Muslim, and Christian holy sites in the Old City and its environs is the one area where a consensus does not yet exist. President Clinton proposed to divide the sovereignty with Palestinians taking the top of the Haram al-Sharif/Temple Mount where the mosques are located and Israel taking the Western Wall of which the Wailing Wall is a part. But Israelis and the Jewish Diaspora are unlikely to accept Palestinian sovereignty on the Temple Mount any more than Palestinians and Muslims could accept Israeli sovereignty there. It would be better to place all the holy sites under a special regime, in which God's sovereignty would be supreme and in which the current temporal administration of the holy sites by the respective religious authorities would be maintained.

3 One of the most effective arguments used by the opponents of Sharon's Gaza disengagement plan was that he was giving up territory and settlements for nothing in return.

Of course, strong arguments would be mounted against outlining American parameters for such an end game. Some will claim that it would be tantamount to imposing a settlement on the parties. But there is an important distinction that would have to be explained and maintained between outlining what the United States' positions will be on these final status issues and attempting to impose those positions on the parties.

Successive presidents, from Carter and Reagan to Clinton and Bush, have already laid out the elements of this end game in one form or another. In particular, at the end of his administration, President Clinton laid out the parameters of a two-state solution that were similar to those just outlined; since then President Bush has articulated his own vision of a two-state solution that includes many of the principles Clinton espoused.[4]

President Bush would need to draw on this bipartisan history in defining the end game. But he would need to take an important step that none of his predecessors contemplated: securing in advance Arab and EU endorsement for the critical compromises the Palestinians would have to make as part of that end game. That would both give the new Palestinian leadership the political cover, and the Israeli people an added inducement, for them both to embrace the American end game principles.

Democracy First?

Increasingly, voices are heard in Washington insisting that the Palestinians first democratize their system of government before the United States make any serious effort to help secure their demands for statehood in the West Bank and Gaza. This idea, first promoted by Natan Sharansky, a member of the right-wing camp that opposes even Sharon's disengagement from Gaza, clearly resonates with a president who has made the pursuit of democracy and freedom the *leitmotiv* of his second term.

In fact, democratization is an idea which falls on fertile Palestinian ground. In the post-Arafat era, the Palestinians want more accountable government for themselves rather than because the United States or Israel insist on it.[5] They have experienced both the impact of a corrupt, tyrannical kleptocracy imposed by Arafat, and the role that an independent judiciary in Israel has played in helping to protect their rights. Under occupation, they have developed a sophisticated civil society, an educated middle class, and in recent years, a serious reform movement. The Palestinians were the ones to insist on presidential elections to choose Arafat's successor, just as they now insist on Legislative Council elections and elections in the ruling Fatah party to introduce real accountability into their government institutions.

Accordingly, there is no need to set democratization as a precondition for active American involvement in peacemaking. The Palestinian democratization process is already under way. Certainly the United States and the international community should give a boost to that process by supporting the establishment of accountable political institutions, transparent economic institutions, and an independent judiciary. But Hamas has already made clear its intention to run in the upcoming elections and its support

---

4 President Bush declared U.S. support for a viable, democratic Palestinian state living alongside a secure Israel in June 2002. In the Roadmap, he endorsed the principle of "ending the occupation that began in 1967." In a subsequent letter of assurance to Prime Minister Sharon, Bush also declared American support for the incorporation of major settlement blocs into Israel and for resolving the Palestinian refugee problem in the State of Palestine rather than in the State of Israel.

5 Sharon actually does not include democratization in his list of demands of the Palestinian Authority. His concern is much more on the need for them to dismantle the terror infrastructure, which may be made more difficult in the short-term by a focus on democratization.

will be greatly strengthened if political liberalization and an anti-corruption drive are not matched by a parallel process that gives hope to Palestinians that they can also achieve freedom from occupation, through negotiations rather than Hamas-led violence and terrorism. In other words, it is essential that democratization and peacemaking go hand-in-hand, to strengthen the forces of moderation on the Palestinian side.

THE SYRIA CARD

One factor that could significantly improve the prospects for achieving progress on Middle East peacemaking would be a parallel effort to resume negotiations on the Syrian and Lebanese tracks. Until recently the option did not exist because President Asad argued that resumption of negotiations with Israel first required progress on the Palestinian track. However, in December 2003, Asad announced publicly that he was ready to begin direct negotiations with the Sharon government without preconditions.[6] Recently, he has repeated that offer, and taken several other steps intended to underscore his seriousness.[7] Asad's apparent flexibility about the basis for restarting negotiations suggests that it would be a relatively straightforward challenge. Moreover, the issues that separate Syria and Israel from a peace deal are much less complicated and much more narrowly focused than those that divide Israelis and Palestinians.[8]

On the Israeli side, however, the challenge is more complicated. Although Israelis are convinced the Syrians want only a "cold peace," they know from long experience that the Syrian state keeps its agreements to the letter, unlike the Palestinians who have done so much to observe them in the breach. Yet, precisely because the

Golan Heights remain tranquil as a result of Syrian adherence to the 1974 Disengagement Agreement, Israelis feel no particular pressure to cede them back. And, in any case, Sharon cannot now contemplate igniting the opposition of the Golan settlers and their supporters at a time when he has his hands full confronting the West Bank and Gaza settlers.

There are several advantages in making resumption of Syrian negotiations part of the broader strategy of Middle East peacemaking:

- Since Syria is the so-called "beating heart of pan-Arabism," its involvement in direct negotiations with Israel would provide political cover for the all-important involvement of other Arab states in the peacemaking effort.

- Since shutting down Syrian support for Palestinian terrorist groups should necessarily be a post-9/11 American requirement for reengagement on the Syrian track, and Asad has already begun to address this demand, it would put pressure on these groups to cease their activities against Israel.

- Syria would have an interest in constraining Hizballah's activities in southern Lebanon and its aggressive support for Palestinian terror groups lest those actions disrupt the negotiations (as they did so often in the past).

- Bringing Syria into the circle of Arab-Israeli peace would remove the last Arab army from the conflict with Israel and solidify Syrian cooperation in the effort to stabilize Iraq. And it would strain the alliance between Syria and Iran—which remains unreconciled to Israel's

---

6 See Asad's interview with Neil MacFarquhar, "Syrian Pressing for Israel Talks," *The New York Times,* Dec 1, 2003.

7 In October 2004, for example, the Ba'th Party Regional Command passed a resolution declaring that peace with Israel was Syria's "strategic choice." Later in the month, Syrian officials announced that they would rebuild the Golan Heights city of Qunaytra as a sign of its peaceful intentions.

8 The essential difference between Asad and Barak during the Clinton era came down to the fate of a 200-meter strip of land on the northeastern foreshores of the Sea of Galilee.

existence—thereby helping efforts to isolate and contain Iran.

The assassination of Rafiq Hariri has of course severely complicated the effort to engage Syria in peace process diplomacy. For the time being, the United States must focus on promoting free and fair elections in Lebanon and the removal of Syrian troops. Yet keeping the door open to Syrian engagement in the peace process as we attempt to close the door on its occupation of Lebanon could help both efforts. Conversely, if we shut both doors we increase the incentive for Syria to unleash Hizballah and Palestinian rejectionist groups to disrupt our efforts and deflect our attention.

PRESIDENTIAL ENVOY FOR MIDDLE EAST PEACEMAKING

The best way to pursue an initiative designed to achieve a settlement of the Arab-Israeli conflict is to announce at an early stage the appointment of a high-level presidential envoy for Middle East peacemaking. While this idea had some currency during the transition, it now seems clear that Secretary of State Condoleezza Rice prefers to do the job herself. This would make sense if she did not have so many other priorities demanding her attention, such as stabilizing Iraq, restoring relations with the European Union, dealing with Iranian and North Korean nuclear proliferation, and managing relations with Russia and China. Henry Kissinger had to make 26 shuttle trips to secure an Israeli-Syrian disengagement agreement; Warren Christopher made 19 Middle East journeys in support of President Clinton's diplomatic efforts; James Baker made 9 trips just to bring the parties together for negotiations at the 1991 Madrid Conference. If President Bush wants to be the peacemaker in the Middle East, he will need a full-time Secretary of State just for that issue alone and that is why he should appoint a high-level presidential Middle East envoy.

The criteria for this appointment are an individual who has, and is seen to have, the ear of the president; has sufficient gravitas to wield influence with Middle East leaders in his/her own right (i.e. more senior than the envoys appointed in Bush's first term); has experience and knowledge in dealing with Arab-Israeli issues and/or negotiating settlements of intense conflicts; and is trusted by the Israelis and respected by the Arabs.

Because the envoy needs to report directly to the president, consideration should be given to locating his/her office in the National Security Council rather than the State Department. The envoy would need to draw on the resources of the State Department's Near East Bureau and other parts of the State Department through officers seconded to the NSC. The envoy would need to consider having a personal representative located in the region, capable of dealing with all the relevant parties to prepare the ground and follow up on the envoy's visits. This would enable the envoy to avoid the dilemma of either devaluing his/her currency by spending too much time in the region, or reducing his/her effectiveness by not spending enough time there.

The president needs to be aware that the envoy cannot substitute for his own personal involvement with Middle Eastern leaders. Peacemaking decisions are necessarily risky business in this part of the world, and politics is very personal for all of the leaders concerned. If they are to take the necessary risks for peace, they will need to know that the president is personally committed to supporting and helping them.

TIMING

The administration should let it be known from the outset that it intends to make Middle East peacemaking a priority in its broader strategy for the Middle East. At the same time, the administration will need to move quickly to take advantage of the opportunities created by Israel's disengagement from Gaza and Arafat's departure from the West Bank. Nevertheless, Iraq will inevitably become the president's first priority. But as he and his advisers begin the process of consultation with European and Middle Eastern leaders about Iraq, he should also discuss his peacemaking strategy with them, putting them on notice that he will be coming to them for support to nurture new Palestinian leadership; help in the Gaza disengagement process; cut external backing for Palestinian terror, especially from Iran; and persuade Israelis of their positive intentions in the end game.[9]

Sharon will be particularly nervous about the president's intentions because he had become comfortable with Bush's earlier backing for his approach. But as he looks to his own reelection bid in the next two years, he will not want to allow any daylight to show between himself and the president, which gives the United States considerable influence with him. It will be essential to reassure the Israeli prime minister that he will continue to be treated as an ally and friend, as we press forward. But he will also need to understand that the president is indeed serious about moving forward.

Accordingly, the first nine-to-twelve months of the Administration should be focused on the Gaza disengagement and the promotion of a capable, responsible, and accountable Palestinian leadership that curbs terror. Behind the scenes the ground should be prepared for a follow-on initiative that would restart the Syrian negotiations and lay out the principles of the end game for the Israeli-Palestinian negotiations as a way of jump-starting implementation of the Roadmap in the West Bank.

Usama bin Laden is reputed to have said, "You Americans have the watches, but we Middle Easterners have the time." This is worth bearing in mind. President Bush will have four years to try to generate a settlement of the Arab-Israeli conflict. That is just as well because no matter how hopeful things may suddenly seem, the Middle East is notorious for confounding expectations and generating unexpected developments (e.g. new elections in Israel or conflict in Lebanon) that would necessarily delay the launching of a new American initiative. But the region has been starved of American peacemaking leadership, the parties have all but exhausted themselves in bloody conflict, Israel is in the process of evacuating settlements, Arafat has now been removed from the equation at a time when the Palestinians are increasingly ready for new leadership, and the Syrians are knocking on the peace door even as they attempt to hold on to Lebanon. A steady and flexible approach in which the administration's first year is spent preparing the ground, the second year is spent in negotiations, and the third and first half of the fourth years are devoted to deal making, might just produce the breakthroughs that seem far off now.

But it is important to conclude with a word of caution. The Bush Administration should be under no illusions. Arab-Israeli peace is one of the most threatening challenges to Islamic extremists. Backed by Iran, they can be expected to do everything possible to thwart our efforts. This calculation must be built in to the Administration's counter-terrorism strategy and its strategy for dealing with Iran.

---

9 Normally the secretary of state would make an early tour of the region and by March–April, the Israeli, Egyptian, and Jordanian leaders would come to Washington.

Saving Iraq:
A Plan For Winning the Peace in 2005

Kenneth M. Pollack

At present, there is no American foreign policy effort in the Middle East—or perhaps in the world—more important than the reconstruction of Iraq. By toppling Saddam Hussein's odious regime and liberating the Iraqi people from his tyranny, the United States took on responsibility for remaking one of the most important and divided Arab states, situated in the midst of one of the world's most economically vital regions. For that reason, the United States cannot afford to fail in Iraq. Washington cannot risk the kind of instability in the Persian Gulf that would likely spread from the collapse of reconstruction there. While there are still aspects of Iraqi society that give hope that Washington can help forge a stable, pluralist, and prosperous Iraq, other features of the nation make it vulnerable to fragmentation, chaos, and civil war.

Thus, Iraq hangs in the balance, and only the United States will be able to determine whether it rises or falls. It is convenient and, to American ears, rhetorically logical to claim that the Iraqis must take reconstruction into their own hands and solve their problems themselves. It is also entirely misguided, at least in the short and medium terms. After 30 years of tyrannical misrule, 12 years of sanctions, and 3 major wars, Iraq

is in ruins. Moreover, Saddam's totalitarianism inculcated a stultifying passivity into the population of Iraq. Saddam did not want Iraqis doing for themselves; he wanted them wholly dependent on Baghdad for even the most minor of decisions. Consequently, Coalition personnel in Iraq routinely note that Iraqis rarely take any action but expect "the authorities" to do it for them—and when they do try to take action, they feel the need for multiple reassurances and permissions before doing so. In short, the Iraqis generally lack both the resources and the attitude to make reconstruction work.

Only the United States has the wherewithal to do so. However, the Bush Administration has created a dilemma for itself. Immediately after the fall of Baghdad, Iraqis looked to the United States to rebuild their country. Most did not particularly like having Americans in charge of their country, but they tolerated the American presence because they recognized their overwhelming need. After 22 months, the United States has mostly worn out its welcome in Iraq. The problem is that Washington has not delivered on its promises; specifically, as far as the Iraqis are concerned, the United States has singularly failed to provide them with day-to-day security, basic services (regular electricity, clean water, gasoline, and other necessities of everyday life), jobs, etc. As a result, growing numbers of Iraqis want the United States out of Iraq altogether, under the logic of "if you are not going to rebuild our country, why are you in it?" But Iraq is far from having the kind of security services, political system, or economic structure that would be able to survive on their own without massive American support.

The failures of the U.S.-led reconstruction effort have been the principal cause of the Iraqi insurgency, and are slowly increasing the risk of all-out civil war. A small but growing minority of Iraqis is concluding that the United States either cannot or will not do what is necessary to make reconstruction work for them, and they are agitating for their countrymen to take matters into their own hands. Throughout southern Iraq, most of the Shi'ite clergy remain committed to reconstruction—if only because Ayatollah Sistani has told them to and because they are deathly afraid of the civil war that all Iraqis expect to erupt if the United States leaves or fails—but they are also quietly building militias, recruiting fighters, and stockpiling arms to defend the local neighborhood and its mosque because they fear that civil war is coming whether they like it or not. And this is the reality for Iraq: that the failure of reconstruction will likely mean chaos and civil war.

No one should be under the impression that Iraq could divide neatly into three pieces. The Kurds have the best chance to establish a unified ministate, and even there it is just unclear that the two great rival militias of the Kurdistan Democratic Party and the Patriotic Union of Kurdistan could co-exist peacefully within a new Kurdish state. The rest of the country would be even worse: southern and western Iraq are patchworks of divided loyalties, ethnic and religious intermingling, and a poverty of leaders capable of commanding large numbers of people. If reconstruction fails, the most likely scenario is for Iraq to shatter into 300 or 3,000 different little pieces, all of them fighting to stay alive—all of them just strong enough to slaughter or beat back their neighbors, but none strong enough to unify the country. No doubt conquerors will arise among them, and one may some day regain control over the entire state, but it would be a long, bloody, and vicious process that would have terrible repercussions for Iraq, the region, and the United States.

The answer to these conundrums can only be that the United States must stay in Iraq for quite some time to come—and in the immediate future, it may have to increase its presence and its involvement in Iraqi affairs—but must be seen by the Iraqis as producing tangible results in doing so. The longer the United States continues on in the same path, maintaining a large presence and a heavy hand in Iraqi affairs without any concomitant improvement in those things most important to the Iraqi people, the worse the situation will become. This means that the Bush Administration needs to reconsider the most fundamental aspects of its approach to Iraqi reconstruction, including security, political reconstitution, and economic development. The Administration would also be well advised to rethink its posture toward the role of the United Nations and Iraq's neighbors in the reconstruction process.

SECURITY: TIME FOR A NEW STRATEGY?

It has become a truism to say that nothing in Iraq will improve meaningfully unless the security situation is radically improved. However, it is no less true for being trite. There are two interrelated components to insecurity in Iraq: the growing and increasingly diverse insurgency against the U.S.-led reconstruction effort and the continuing lawlessness that permeates much of the society. There has been a slight improvement with regard to the latter problem, as well as a considerable shift in its nature. Today, there is less random crime and more organized crime; there are fewer opportunistic muggings and more planned burglaries; fewer random kidnappings of young girls off the streets for sex and more deliberate kidnappings of wealthy Iraqis for money. Of course, the simple fact that 21 months after the fall of Baghdad these problems of widespread crime still persist is an embarrassment to the United States and a frustration for the Iraqi people. It persuades more and more Iraqis that the United States lacks either the capability or the willingness to deal with the problems. This in turn reinforces their desire to have the United States out and to turn instead to other Iraqis—principally meaning local militias and insurgent groups—to solve their problems instead.

Although for the first 12–16 months following the fall of Baghdad the lawlessness was the more debilitating element of insecurity in Iraq, the steady worsening of the insurgency is now threatening to reverse these priorities. The Bush Administration (and the interim government led by Iyad Allawi) wrongly paints the insurgency as being the product largely of foreign-born Salafi jihadists, Iranian agents, and former regime loyalists. While all of these groups have contributed to a greater or lesser extent to the insurgency (the Iranians least of all), the greatest threat that the United States faces in Iraq is that the insurgency is drawing upon an ever greater base of support throughout a wide range of Iraqi society. Indeed, the two aspects of insecurity reinforce each other as the insurgents often engage in organized crime, and the persistent lawlessness turns increasing numbers of Iraqis toward the insurgents and militias as an alternative that might be able to do for them what the United States cannot.

The fact that only a minority of Iraqis support the insurgency is irrelevant compared to the growth in the size of that minority, the depth of their commitment, and the diversity of the base. Today, the insurgency has deep roots within the tribal Sunni Arab community of western Iraq. That segment of Iraqi society never favored the U.S. liberation, and has always believed that the United States intended to overturn Iraq's power structure so that they—who had been on top for the previous 80 years—would be oppressed by the Shi'ite majority whom they had oppressed themselves during that period. Unfortunately, repeated American miscues have simply reinforced that conviction. As a result, in towns like Fallujah, Haditha, Ramadi, Rutbah, Habbaniyah, Samarra, and elsewhere in western Iraq, the insurgents are generally seen as popular champions fighting against the imperialist Americans and their Shi'ite (and Kurdish) puppets.

The surprising strength of Muqtada al-Sadr's Mahdi Army in the battles throughout southern Iraq in April 2004 and again in July point to another aspect of the insurgency—its (slowly) growing popularity among the Shi'a. Very few Iraqis, and very few Shi'a, like Sadr or respect him enough to do his bidding out of a sense of obligation. Instead, his support is drawn largely from two sources: his ability to provide the basic security and services that the United States and the interim Iraqi government cannot, and his open opposition to the United States. The former illustrates the danger of allowing insecurity to persist, driving people into the arms of local warlords who (following the model Hizballah developed in Lebanon) are eager to show them that they can provide the tangible benefits that the Americans cannot. The latter is, in some ways, even more dangerous. Many people joined Sadr's forces in openly resisting the Coalition during the summer of 2004 not because they liked what he stood *for*—public opinion polls have demonstrated consistent Iraqi aversion to the Iranian-style theocracy he advocates—but because they like what he stands *against*. From the earliest days after the fall of Baghdad, he has demanded that the United States vacate Iraq, and as Iraqis have soured on the U.S. presence because of our many mistakes over the previous 18 months, they have sweetened on Sadr's message.

In general, the United States has consistently exaggerated the role of individuals (Abu Musab al-Zarqawi, Saddam Hussein, Sadr) in the insurgency. All have some degree of importance. None are so important that their elimination would lead to a meaningful change in the course of the conflict, as witnessed by the continuing deterioration even after Saddam's capture and his sons' deaths. Likewise, the United States has consistently exaggerated the importance of various events and dates to the insurgency—things like the June 30 handover and now the January elections. Insurgent attacks have worsened in a straight-line progression over the past 21 months; that trend has been wholly determined by the growth in the capabilities, support, and freedom of action of the insurgents, not Washington's calendar of events.

The insurgents want to drive the United States out of Iraq, undermine the reconstruction, and dissuade Iraqis from participating in the reconstruction effort; they attack wherever and whenever they can based on their own demands, not on an artificial timeline or events that are irrelevant to them. Moreover, the growth of support among segments of Iraqi society for the insurgents, as well as their rapidly maturing skills, means that the role of the foreign jihadists is of much less significance than it once was. Initially, the foreigners were important to the insurgency because they brought training, experience, know-how, and ideology that the Iraqis lacked. At this point, the pupils are getting to the point where they know enough that they need little help from their erstwhile teachers.

What all of this suggests is that we may be approaching the point where our initial approach to security—and, more importantly, the approach to security that the United States *should have* employed after the invasion, both

of which focused on a post-conflict stabilization model—may no longer be feasible. Increasingly, we face a full-blown insurgency supported by a sizable minority of the populace and in control of considerable swathes of territory. It suggests that the United States may need to shift to a true counterinsurgency (COIN) strategy, which in turn has fairly dramatic implications for the reconstruction.

The key principle of the current, broad approach to security (the post-conflict stabilization approach) is that it attempts to pacify the entire country more or less simultaneously, preventing the insurgents from securing safe havens and focusing on political and economic progress across the board to help the country "shed" the violence by undermining the key claim of the insurgents (and would-be warlords) that only they can provide security and basic services.

The problem is that, right from the start, there has been an imbalance between resources and strategy. The United States never mustered the forces to successfully pacify the entire country. Because it was unwilling to commit sufficient American forces and unable to secure significant foreign forces for that mission, the Bush Administration rushed the formation and training of Iraqi forces, with the predictable result that they often collapsed under the slightest pressure. Today, the Administration has even less prospect of garnering large foreign contributions and has had to go back and start building new Iraqi security forces from scratch. In short, the Bush Administration never provided the resources needed for the ambitious objectives it adopted. The obvious alternative would be to scale back our objectives to a level commensurate with our actual capabilities; a traditional COIN approach would allow us to do so.

A true COIN strategy, usually referred to as a "spreading oil stain" or "spreading ink spot" approach, would instead focus on securing enclaves[1] or protected areas (Kurdistan, most of the predominantly Shi'ite southeast, Baghdad, and a number of other major urban centers, along with the oilfields and some other vital economic facilities) while, initially, leaving much of the countryside outside Kurdistan and the Shi'ite southeast to the insurgents.[2] The Coalition would consolidate its security forces within those areas, thereby greatly improving the ratio of security personnel to civilians, and allowing a major effort to secure these areas to allow local economic and political development to thrive. The Coalition would likewise redirect its political efforts and economic resources solely into the secured areas—both to ensure that they prosper and because those would be the only areas where it would be worth investing in the short run.

Such a strategy would therefore mean forgoing such things as national elections or rebuilding the entire power grid, because they would be impossible in a situation where the Coalition forces had abdicated control over large areas of the country. The concentrated security focus should allow local economic and political developments to make meaningful progress, which in turn should turn around public opinion within these protected areas (making the Iraqis living in the enclaves more willing to support the reconstruction effort and, hopefully, making those Iraqis outside the protected areas more desirous of experiencing the same benefits).

Once these areas were secured, and as additional Iraqi security forces were trained or foreign forces brought in, they would be slowly expanded to include additional communities—hence the metaphor of the spreading oil stain. In every case, the Coalition would focus the same security, political, and economic resources on each new community brought into the pacified zone. If implemented properly, a true counterinsurgency approach can succeed in winning back the entire country. However, it means ceding control over large swathes of it at first and taking much longer before Iraq will be seen as a stable, unified, pluralist state. Nevertheless, it may be the only option open to us if, as is the case at present, the U.S.-led coalition cannot control large parts of the country and cannot even keep the peace in those areas where it can operate.

The critical test of whether the point has been reached where the United States should consider shifting to a true COIN strategy will be the outcome of the Administration's campaign to pacify Samarra, Fallujah, and other key towns in the Sunni triangle in the first six months after the January 2005 elections for the Iraqi transitional government. As every American military officer readily explained, taking these towns was the easy part; securing them so that the insurgents could not re-establish themselves there at a later date was the hard part—and by far the most important part if the post-conflict stabilization model is going to work. If this campaign is largely successful, it will suggest that the current post-conflict stabilization approach to security is still a feasible strategy. If it fails, it will suggest that the current approach is no longer viable and that the United States might be best served by shifting to a COIN strategy.

---

1 "Enclave" is something of a misnomer as it suggests a relatively small area. Because of the considerable residual support for reconstruction among the Shi'ite majority and the large Kurdish minority, these "enclaves" would actually constitute a very significant percentage of the entire country.

2 On counterinsurgency strategy, see for instance Keith B. Bickel, *Mars Learning: The Marine Corps' Development of Small Wars Doctrine, 1915–1940* (Westview, 2000); Andrew Krepinevich, *The Army and Vietnam* (Johns Hopkins University Press, 1988); Ronald Schaffer, *The United States Marine Corps Small Wars Manual, 1940*, Reprinted edition (Sunflower University Press, 1996); United States Marine Corps, *Operations Against Guerrilla Forces*, Reprint of the 1962 Marine Corps manual (Fredonia Press, 2004); Mao Zedong, *On Guerrilla Warfare*, Translated by Samuel B. Griffith II (University of Illinois Press, 2000).

MATCHING ENDS AND MEANS

Another obvious issue for the security dimension of reconstruction will be increasing the numbers of properly trained military and other security forces within the country. Although this would be highly useful for any effort to stabilize the country (including a true COIN strategy) it is probably vital to a continued effort to employ the current post-conflict stabilization strategy.

At present, the Coalition simply does not have the forces to secure the entirety of the country. There are three possible sources of additional troops:

- ***The Iraqis.*** Major General David Petraeus was charged several months ago with starting over again—virtually from scratch—to train Iraqi military forces capable of keeping the peace within the country. Petraeus made clear at the outset that he expects this to be a 3–5-year job, reflecting the time needed to properly vet, train, equip, monitor, organize, and shake down loyal, professional units capable of standing up to the challenges of security in Iraq. He is absolutely right to focus on the quality of personnel, not the numbers; Washington's obsession with the reverse has cost us dearly since the fall of Baghdad. While some Iraqi units will likely be available sooner than others, we should not count on significant numbers of fully able Iraqi forces for months if not years. The Administration's publicly proclaimed numbers of trained troops are disingenuous at best. They reflect forces that have not been properly vetted or trained, but simply have been put through courses as brief as eight weeks before being added to the Pentagon tally. These forces have frequently shown themselves to be either disloyal or incapable of handling the mission; last April, as many as half of those Iraqi security personnel committed to fighting the Mahdi Army refused to fight, fled, or joined the opposition. Moreover, rushing the training program would be dangerous. It was the Administration's effort to rush the initial training that led to the failure of the first batch of Iraqi security forces during the spring of 2004. The United States must give the new units of Iraqi troops time before it puts them in the line of fire. To do otherwise would be to court yet another disaster.

- ***The United States.*** At present, Washington is maintaining 135–140,000 troops in Iraq. These have been adequate so far to prevent the country from falling apart, but inadequate for reconstruction to gain traction. It would be possible to increase this force to roughly 180,000 troops for a period of 6–12 months should we choose to do so. However, the cost would be to undermine the rotational system set up by the Army to sustain a 120–140,000-man force in Iraq for the foreseeable future. Consequently, such a ramping up could only be a short-term expedient. After the 6–12-month surge, troop levels would have to drop dramatically (to levels well below the current level of 140,000) or risk badly burning out personnel, destroying retention and enlistment rates, increasing casualties, and undermining morale. Thus, this can only be a short-term step and would have to be part of a larger effort that could use the 6–12-month window it would create to put in place other mechanisms to bring long-term security.

- ***The Allies.*** For a combination of reasons, it will be highly difficult for Washington to secure additional forces from countries other than the United States and Iraq. Many are still angry at the Administration for its handling of both the prewar diplomacy and the postwar reconstruction. Others face hostile publics and are daunted by a deteriorating security situation. Moreover, there are only a handful of countries with the kind of military establishments that could provide significant contributions to the effort.

These considerations suggest two different scenarios. First, to the extent that a post-conflict stabilization strategy is still viable, the Administration may want to adopt a two-pronged strategy. This would consist of plussing up the U.S. military presence in Iraq to roughly 180,000 troops for as long as Washington could keep them there—hopefully 12 months or more. This increase could allow the Administration to bring greater stability to important parts of the country. It could use that 6–12-month window to give a number of Iraqi units the time they needed to become loyal, capable elements that could supplement U.S. forces, and convince skittish European (and Asian) populations that Iraq is no longer as dangerous as it once was. The goal would be to have available foreign and Iraqi forces that could then take over for the American units when they need to be withdrawn. If this succeeded, it would stabilize Iraq, result in greater allied involvement, and produce a significantly smaller American presence on the ground within a period of about 12 months.

On the other hand, and particularly if the military developments of the next six months demonstrate that the post-conflict stabilization scenario is no longer viable and continued recalcitrance on the part of our allies means that we cannot secure any additional contributions of troops, then the United States should opt for a traditional COIN strategy. The Administration certainly would benefit enormously from greater allied commitments even were it to adopt a COIN strategy (for political and diplomatic as well as military reasons), but they are probably not as vital to a COIN campaign as they would be to a continued post-conflict stabilization approach. And by drawing the ring of protected areas tightly around those zones capable of being pacified and defended by the existing Coalition and Iraqi forces, it would reduce the need for large numbers of additional troops—American, Iraqi, or allied. The United States would then allow the oil stains to spread at the rate that

additional trained Iraqi troops became available, maintaining the current U.S. force levels as the backbone of the effort for the foreseeable future.

TACTICAL CHANGES

In addition, there is still room for improvement in the tactical approach employed by Coalition armed forces in meeting the challenge of security in Iraq for Iraqis. Some progress is already being made on a number of these issues in response to 21 months of criticism from insiders and outsiders alike. However, in every case, there is more that needs to be done.

Make Patrolling the Priority Over Raiding. Raids against suspected insurgents—or their supporters—rarely result in meaningful accomplishments and often backfire and alienate innocent Iraqis, their friends, relatives, and neighbors. On the other hand, as the British learned in Northern Ireland, as the Israelis learned in the occupied territories, and as in every other successful COIN campaign, having men patrolling on the streets is absolutely vital to success. The people need to see foot soldiers constantly—to feel safe, to feel that they have security personnel they can turn to, to get comfortable with them, and eventually to point out who the bad guys are. British veterans of Northern Ireland in particular point out that over time, constant foot patrols are the key to obtaining the intelligence needed to actually identify real insurgents. Foot patrols are obviously dangerous and increase the risk to personnel, but they are vital to accomplishing the mission that our forces are in Iraq to accomplish.

Mixed Patrols. As trained Iraqi security personnel become available, they need to be married up with American and other Coalition troops. Twenty-two months after the fall of Baghdad, Iraqis are increasingly unhappy with a heavy American military presence, while simultaneously being deeply distressed that the U.S. military is not doing more to attend to their security needs.

These conflicting views present a major challenge for the United States. The best solution seems to be mixed patrols. With mixed patrols, Iraqis can feel assured by the presence of the Coalition troops that the security forces are there to protect them—not to shake them down, rob them, kidnap their daughters, or turn them over to the insurgents, as has too often been the case with the initial wave of untrained and unvetted Iraqi forces thrown into the fray—but they can also see Iraqi troops as full partners and so assuage their feelings of humiliation. In addition, the Iraqis are better able than U.S. troops to talk to the civilians, resulting in reduced problems and increased information gathering. U.S. units in Iraq are increasingly employing such mixed patrols and where they are, they are enjoying considerable success.

Protect Iraqis Participating in Reconstruction. In part because the United States has made force protection an overriding priority (to the detriment of other mission objectives like pacifying the country), and in part because they are a more important target, the insurgents have increasingly attacked other Iraqis participating in reconstruction—interim government officials, security personnel, and businessmen working with the Coalition—as well as the oil, power, and water infrastructure. The goal of these attacks is to dissuade Iraqis from participating in the reconstruction. This is a dire threat to the success of reconstruction. It has had a chilling effect on considerable segments of a population that for cultural and historical reasons is mostly passive to begin with. In this case as well, the solution requires the United States to be more willing to put its own foot soldiers in harm's way, to protect key facilities and personnel. Obviously, this risks greater U.S. casualties, but it is absolutely critical. A major complaint of the Iraqis is that U.S. forces are only interested in protecting themselves, not the Iraqis; the United States must make the Iraqis feel that it is doing everything it can to protect them.

More Infantry, More Civil-Affairs Personnel, and More Interpreters. While there are shortfalls across the board, these are probably the three most pressing needs. We need infantrymen capable of going on foot patrols, protecting Iraq's daily economic activities, and guarding Iraqi facilities and even personnel. Currently, there are far too few. A major element of this problem is the Army's emphasis on specialization and the limited amount of regular combat training most Army personnel receive. In this area the Marines do a much better job, with the result that Marine units have many more personnel capable of performing pure infantry missions than comparable Army units. Similarly, we have far too few civil-affairs personnel in Iraq. Wherever they are located, they generally have the Midas touch, but there just are not enough of them for a country as big as Iraq.

Finally, the United States desperately needs more Arabic-language speakers in Iraq. Part of the solution to this problem is to marry up fully vetted and trained Iraqi units with Coalition units. However, the Bush Administration may also want to begin a major effort to recruit among the Arab-American community (who remain distressingly uninvolved in U.S. political life) to bring them over to Iraq in a special category of service (perhaps through AID or some other part of the State Department) for short-term stints as translators. It would demonstrate the Administration's determination to be both creative and proactive, would help address a vital need, and would demonstrate the Administration's desire to reach out to an important constituency that has generally felt alienated from their government.

Institute a Centralized System for Learning Lessons and Disseminating Them Quickly. One of the greatest problems of the military's efforts at reconstruction in Iraq is that units (particularly civil-affairs teams) are sent out into Iraq with little instruction and little idea of what they need to accomplish and what has worked (and failed) elsewhere in the country. The United States should quickly establish a central office in Iraq to gather lessons from teams in the field, assimilate those experiences into general guidance, and then distribute it back out to the field. This is a fairly simple and obvious step, but it desperately needs doing.

THE POLITICAL SECTOR

With the elections for the transitional national assembly out of the way, Washington and Baghdad must turn to a range of short- and long-term problems hindering Iraq's political development. Those that stand out as probably the most important over the course of the next year include shepherding Iraq's process for adopting a new constitution, reaching out to its alienated Sunni tribal community, working out a workable power-sharing arrangement, and jump-starting the rather moribund process of democratic education and institution building at the grassroots level across the country.

ENSURING THE WRITING OF A FEASIBLE CONSTITUTION

Over the course of 2005, the Iraqis are expected to draft, vote on, adopt, and then hold elections under the auspices of a new constitution. Although it is the least immediate problem, it is also the most important. The nature of the constitution is critical to the stability of a nation. The United States nearly failed as a nation because of the faults of the Articles of Confederation, but has prospered thanks to the constitution that replaced them. Similarly, Germany under the Weimar system was a never-ending series of catastrophes, but has proven extremely stable under the postwar system. This is not to suggest that constitutions are all-important, only that they do exert considerable influence on a country's future, and this is particularly the case for a nation like Iraq that is badly divided already and with historical pressures for fragmentation.

Getting Iraq's constitution right will likely be critical to its prosperity and stability, and possibly even to its survival.

Unfortunately, the proportional representation system to which Washington acquiesced for the January 2005 elections could easily be disastrous for Iraq if codified in a new constitution. All party leaders want proportional representation because it rewards party loyalty and favors weak national parties over strong individual candidates. It is only natural that Iraq's party leaders favored it, especially given how little popular support they have throughout the country.

But a bigger problem with proportional representation is that it polarizes the political system. By requiring would-be leaders to get elected as part of party slates, it reinforces party loyalty and encourages parties to highlight their differences, thereby pushing to the extremes. It also rewards the fringes of a society at the expense of the moderates: because voting is not done locally, a would-be radical simply needs to find enough radical supporters across the entire population to get elected, rather than having to find a concentration of them in a specific geographic area. Fringe voters can vote for fringe candidates who represent extreme views, or simply single issues. Thus, proportional representation results in badly fragmented parliaments where tiny extremist parties can pull larger moderate blocks to their extreme positions because the moderates invariably lack the parliamentary majorities necessary to rule and so must build coalitions that include radical groups.

This is why in deeply polarized societies—like Israel today or Weimar Germany in the 1930s—proportional representation paralyzes government and undermines domestic stability. For this reason, proportional representation is the worst system imaginable for Iraq. A country that is already badly polarized and possessing only unrepresentative parties does not need an electoral system that promotes greater factionalism and polarization and will allow unrepresentative parties to solidify their control over power.[3]

Building Democracy from the Bottom Up

One of the lessons of the various postwar reconstruction operations undertaken over the past 15 years—as well as the many transitions from authoritarianism to democracy that so many nations have experienced since World War II—is that democracy does best when it is allowed to grow from the grassroots level upward, rather than being imposed from the top. Democracy is about empowering the people. Thus, it is self-evident that it cannot function properly if the people do not understand how the system works or what their responsibilities will be. It cannot work if there are no institutions to help organize people and help them accomplish what they need at local levels, without constant recourse to petitioning the central government. It cannot work if leaders cannot emerge from the populace itself, through a process of working their way up the rungs of the system, gaining experience and notoriety as they do. Nor can democracy work if the putative leaders, even if they are chosen in fair and free elections, do not actually represent the people who chose them.

In the first six months after the fall of Baghdad, the United States did a creditable job of attempting to educate Iraqis about democracy and to build local organizations, political parties, and local councils charged with administering towns and neighborhoods. Unfortunately, that effort was then largely aborted with the formation of the Iraqi Governing Council, which (along with the Coalition Provisional Authority) emphasized the centralization of authority in Baghdad and shifted resources to a top-down approach. Indeed, the proportional representation system is one of the fruits of this mistaken shift.

At this late date it will be hard to undo all of the damage done so far, and it is impossible to start over again and do it right. Building a democratic system from the ground up takes a great deal of time, and having squandered nearly the first two years of reconstruction, the United States no longer has time as a luxury. Nevertheless, it is still critical for the United States and the new transitional Iraqi government to work together and with the international community to make a much greater effort in this area.

In particular, the United States and Iraq could benefit greatly from having greater participation from the United Nations. This is one of those areas where the United Nations has access to personnel more experienced in these sorts of activities than does the United States. We would need to create a process of educating Iraqis across the country about democracy as well as the mechanics of representative government and these specific elections. We would need to help new political parties organize and establish themselves. We would need to allow the bottom-up process of building democratic institutions—which has enjoyed considerable success in some parts of Iraq—to continue to develop and to spread across the country.

Power Sharing

Today, Iraq's Kurds, Shi'ite Arabs, and Sunni Arabs are increasingly polarized, threatening to

---

3 The best system for Iraq would probably be some sort of direct, geographic representation. Geographic representation favors the individual candidate over the party, thus allowing the emergence of strong, popular figures. Moreover, it emphasizes compromise within the legislative process. Candidates from districts representing mixed populations have a tremendous incentive to find solutions that will secure the support of all of their constituents. Thus, while proportional representation pushes parliamentarians toward the extremes to demonstrate the differences between the parties, geographic representation pushes parliamentarians toward the center. And Iraq desperately needs a political system that will encourage compromise and centripetal forces. A compromise—proportional representation by province—would be a second-best but possibly feasible alternative.

tear apart the political system. The United States must address that problem promptly, and create a process that will allow for its solution over the long term.

The Kurds would prefer to be independent, but before the invasion they had reconciled themselves to being autonomous—although there was obviously going to be considerable debate about what "autonomy" would look like. However, the deepening problems in the rest of Iraq have pushed Kurds in the direction of ever greater "autonomy" and even outright independence. In private, leading Kurds will argue that the United States is making a mess in the center and the south of the country, and asking why they would want to be part of such a state. Unfortunately, they have a point.

As noted earlier, the Americans have alienated the Sunni Arabs from the process of political reconstitution. The arbitrary and excessive U.S. program of de-Ba'thification, coupled with the disbanding of the army, struck most deeply at tribal Sunnis. In this case, the problem is among the officers, who were generally important members of their tribes. They once had dignity, power, wealth, and patronage, and have been stripped of all that. Not surprisingly, many have gone home and either joined the insurgency or encouraged their sons and nephews to do so.

In addition to humiliating many once powerful Sunni officers, the disbanding of Iraq's army and security services also put a lot of lower-class Sunnis out of work. Although the Shi'a dominated the rank and file of the army, Sunni tribesmen dominated the lower rungs of the Republican Guard and the internal security forces, and these men are now unemployed and easy recruits for the insurgents. What is more, after forcing the tribal Sunnis out of the old government, the United States largely excluded them from the new government. Moreover, the tribal shaykhs formerly depended on power and payments from Baghdad, which have not been forthcoming from the United States (understandably, given both American values and intentions).

Finally, the Shi'a are terrified that they are going to be deprived once again of their demographic right to dominate the Iraqi government. Many still do not trust the United States—which did nothing for them in the past, and is the long-time ally of the Sunni states of Saudi Arabia, Kuwait, Jordan, and Turkey. And many continue to think in traditional Middle Eastern patronage terms, whereby those who dominate the political system get to apportion the country's economic wealth to their constituents. The Shi'a suffered under such a system for 80 years (arguably longer) and they believe that now is their turn at the trough.

It is also important to keep in mind that the Shi'a are themselves badly fragmented. Ayatollah Ali al-Sistani speaks for the Shi'a only to the extent that there is no one else who can, and he is generally careful to speak only on issues about which the bulk of the community is united. However, there are deep divisions among the different Shi'ite militias and nascent parties, and from town to town and neighborhood to neighborhood.

All of these problems point to the pressing need for a power-sharing arrangement. At present, there is a rough compromise, embodied in the Transitional Administrative Law (TAL). This may or may not be the "right" solution for Iraq, but at present it is not accepted by the Shi'ite or Sunni Arab communities, and from America's perspective, that—not the specific provisions—is the problem. If Iraq is going to develop a new, pluralist political system, it is going to have to have a power-sharing arrangement to which all of the parties have agreed, if only grudgingly— and that means tackling all of these issues.

Obviously, this is going to be very difficult to solve. However, time can help heal these wounds. Time should allow the United States to ameliorate a series of immediate, tangible problems (such as energy and unemployment; see below). This should, in turn, make political leaders on all sides more willing to sit down and discuss power sharing and be more amenable to compromise.

With time and a smart new approach to reconstruction, we should be able to stabilize the rest of the country, revive the economy, and start a more realistic process of political development that will make being a part of Iraq seem less unpalatable to many Kurds. It should also allow for the emergence of more reasonable leaders willing to compromise, especially among the Sunni and Shi'ite Arab populations. It should allow us to gain the trust of the Shi'a, and convince the Sunnis that our goal is not to reduce them to the same kind of misery that they inflicted on the Shi'a.

Thus, the Administration must simultaneously begin a process of power-sharing discussions to try to convince all sides that their concerns on this matter are being addressed, while simultaneously postponing other major political developments to remove the pressures to resolve the power-sharing differences created by artificial deadlines.

Ultimately, this power-sharing arrangement will have to be enshrined in the new constitution, but the more that the United States can do to mitigate the pressures on the various groups, the better the long-term outcome may be. If that requires postponing the drafting and referendum on the new constitution, it would be a small price to pay for ensuring that Iraq has a workable constitution that all Iraqis can accept.

Addressing the Sunni Population

The United States is also going to have to do a better job with Iraq's Sunni community, particularly the tribal Sunnis. As noted, they feel completely alienated and have become a geographically large base of support for the various insurgent groups. The State Department and uniformed services are

doing a much better job of reaching out to them in recent months, but there is still more to be done.

A short-term approach and a long-term approach are now needed. The short-term approach is to reach out to the tribal shaykhs, largely as Saddam did, and again offer to provide them with resources if they will "assist with security"—i.e., stop attacking the roads, power lines, oil pipelines, and Coalition forces in their territory and prevent other groups from doing the same. The payments do not necessarily have to be cash, like Saddam's, but the United States, too, needs to find ways to provide resources that will give the tribal shaykhs and their people an incentive to cooperate. This can come in the form of goods, construction equipment or funding for projects, or even the projects themselves. It can come by "deputizing" tribal military leaders, enlisting their personnel in an Iraqi security force (probably the National Guard, which is locally based), and then paying them for their service. The key is to start meeting with the shaykhs and convincing them that if they cooperate, there will be resources and other benefits for them and their followers.

The longer-term approach will involve repairing the deeper psychological damage created by Saddam's misrule and Washington's own initial mistakes. The United States needs to begin a long process of education among Sunni tribesmen (indeed, all across Iraq) that will make them understand the Administration's vision of the new Iraq and their role in it. For instance, the United States needs them to understand that in a system where the rule of law prevails they will not have to fear being oppressed by the Shi'a as they oppressed the Shi'a themselves for at least 80 years. Similarly, the United States needs to persuade them that while they will no longer enjoy the privileged position they had under Saddam, and so will no longer be *relatively* better off than the rest of the country, if the reconstruction succeeds, Iraq will be so much more prosperous than it was under Saddam that in *absolute* terms, they will be much better off.

Finally, the United States must also help the Sunnis develop new political institutions. Here the need may actually be even more pressing than it is for the rest of the country. The Kurds have their two great parties. For the present, the Shi'a at least have Ayatollah Sistani and the Hawza of Najaf—although that, too, is an imperfect vehicle for expressing their true political aspirations. But the Sunnis have nothing. Their principal political institution was the Ba'th party and it has been proscribed, along with all of its senior members. Consequently, the United States is going to have to help them create new, progressive political institutions that will allow their voices to be heard. Even in these, the Sunni tribesmen cannot predominate, and should have no more political power than their demographic weight, but they cannot be excluded entirely as they effectively have been so far.

ECONOMIC DEVELOPMENT

One of the most important positives the United States still has going for it in Iraq is that even after 22 months of missteps by Washington, the Iraqi people remain committed to the process of reconstruction and hopeful that it will work—even though they are increasingly skeptical that the United States will be the one to do so. This public support is absolutely vital to reconstruction: as long as it persists, success is still possible. Once it evaporates, the possibility of success likely will disappear with it. However, this perception probably will not persist forever and it is impossible to know when it will vanish. Public-opinion polls have demonstrated steadily eroding confidence, even though in an absolute sense it remains high. It may be that the erosion will not proceed in a linear fashion but will nose-dive at some unforeseen point in the future. Consequently, the United States needs to move quickly to shore up public support in reconstruction.

PROVIDING TANGIBLE BENEFITS FAST

The most pressing need is for jobs. Iraq's unemployment problems remain staggering because the United States has done a poor job disbursing the funds Congress appropriated for a range of make-work programs. Within the next six months, many of those programs will finally be inaugurated, and that should help, but it definitely will not solve the problem. It is well recognized that massive Iraqi unemployment has fueled Iraq's security problems both directly and indirectly. Washington would do well to build on whatever these programs are able to accomplish in the next few months: the more the United States can create jobs, the more it will improve Iraqi morale, both by getting disgruntled young men off the streets and by creating a sense that the United States is finally addressing the problems of the Iraqi people.

Another consistent problem has been the provision of basic services, particularly electricity and fuel (including gasoline for cars). Although American mistakes have contributed to these problems, the real cause is the decrepit state of Iraq's infrastructure coupled with insurgent attacks, sabotage, and widespread looting. Over the past 22 months, the Coalition has made valiant efforts to rectify these problems as well, and they are slowly improving, albeit not fast enough to satisfy Iraqis who believe they should have been fixed six months ago or more.

Yet a third pressing problem worth highlighting has been the failure of Iraq's economy to begin to rebound. Here, crime and lawlessness are the principal problems. Insecurity means that goods have difficulty traveling along roads because they are often hijacked and stolen. It means factories get vandalized or even robbed in the middle of the day. It means that owners and entrepreneurs can lose their capital and their investments overnight. It means that many of Iraq's wealthy— those who should be taking the risks on their own country to revive its economy—are increasingly targeted for kidnapping by local criminal rings.

At the very least, the United States is going to have to have a plan to start addressing these issues quickly. The potential risk of failing to do so is the final erosion of Iraqi public opinion. The remarkable resilience of Iraqis' faith in the future is the most important thing we have going for us in Iraq, but it will not remain forever, and the two factors that most threaten that optimism are insecurity and related economic problems. The Administration must initiate programs to deal with both sets of issues right away.

DECENTRALIZATION

One important issue that should be addressed is decentralizing economic development and its funding. There are two interacting sets of obstacles here, one Iraqi and one American.

The Iraqi set of obstacles stems from a combination of Arab societal norms reinforced by Saddam's totalitarianism, which has left much of Iraqi society passive and even fearful of taking initiative. In response to these stimuli, Iraq became a debilitatingly over-centralized state over the past 30 years. Thanks to these cultural factors and Saddam's insistence that every minor decision be referred to Baghdad, most Iraqis expect all decisions (often even the most trivial) to be made in Baghdad, and all economic activity tends to flow to Baghdad and then out from it in some way, shape, or form.

This was further exacerbated by various American mistakes. Because the Administration did not have enough people to fully handle the reconstruction of Iraq properly (a separate issue from not having enough troops to secure the country), the Coalition Provisional Authority, too, tended to centralize its personnel in Baghdad and insist that issues be referred down to Baghdad. Some members of the original Governing Council were determined to control all of Iraq's economic activities not just to line their own pockets, but also to use it to buy patronage. The overall result has been that too much of Iraq's political and economic activity is flowing through either the American or the Iraqi political hubs in Baghdad.

Consequently, one of the challenges of reconstruction is getting resources directly into the hands of the Iraqi people, bypassing Baghdad and cutting out much of the U.S. bureaucracy. At present, far too much U.S. aid and Iraqi wealth is blocked by this set of mutually reinforcing bottlenecks. It is critical to take steps such as expanding the U.S. AID program run by the Research Triangle Institute that provides grants directly to local Iraqi councils for infrastructure development; creating a pool of capital to offer micro-loans to Iraqi small businesses; and "privatizing" Iraqi trade (something that is already happening as a result of enterprising Iraqis, but that needs to be institutionalized and regulated).

A related matter has been the Administration's over-reliance on big American firms to handle much of the contracting in Iraq. This makes sense from a bureaucratic perspective but has been bad for reconstruction. Again, it means that resources are not going directly to Iraqis. Indeed, far too much of the funds in each contract stay here in the United States or are directed to subsidiaries in other countries than actually get into Iraq. Whatever graft there is in Halliburton's dealings in Iraq is actually secondary compared to the damage done because so little of the money awarded to Halliburton for a contract actually gets spent in Iraq.

Unfortunately, providing immediate relief from pressing economic problems is only part of the challenge. The Administration also will have to ensure that Iraq experiences economic growth. This is an enormously complicated issue. Nevertheless, it is worth highlighting some of the issues that must be part of such an effort. First,

Iraq's oil production and export systems need a dramatic overhaul to render current (or higher) production levels sustainable well into the future. This process has already started. However, it has been repeatedly sidetracked, both by insurgent attacks and by the need to make short-term fixes to deal with immediate problems. In addition, Iraq's economy needs to be diversified, with oil revenues being used to improve public infrastructure and educate a new generation of Iraqis to become workers and entrepreneurs in a new Iraq firmly embedded within the global economy.

THE UNITED NATIONS

Although it has largely faded from the headlines, there are still important roles to be played by the United Nations. Moreover, greater UN involvement could help pave the way for greater allied contributions. For both of these reasons, the United States should make an effort to engage the United Nations more fully in the reconstruction of Iraq.

At the most basic level, it remains the case that the United Nations, through its various agencies, can call upon a vast network of personnel and resources vital to various aspects of nation-building. One of the greatest problems the United States has faced is that it simply does not have enough people who know how to do all of the things necessary to rebuild the political and economic system of a shattered nation. The United States has not tried to do so since at least Vietnam—if not South Korea, Germany, and Japan. The United Nations, by contrast, has worked with thousands of people who have such skills in Cambodia, Bosnia, Kosovo, East Timor, Afghanistan, and elsewhere. If the United Nations asks those people to help in Iraq, they are quite likely to come, whereas they have largely been unwilling to answer the same call from the Bush Administration for the past 22 months. The ability to tap into a much bigger network of people with desperately needed skills, by itself, is a crucial virtue of the United Nations.

There is also the need for UN cover at the top of the reconstruction pyramid. So far, the interim Iraqi government and the U.S. embassy have not publicly clashed on anything, and so the current arrangement has "worked" so far. But it is unclear that this will always be true: one can postulate a multitude of scenarios in which an Iraqi government—this one or another—will see it in its best interests to disagree with the United States, and then the U.S. ambassador will be in a very weak position to try to prevent the Iraqis from doing as they please, even if it is deleterious to the United States and/or Iraq. This raises again the need for a UN-authorized high commissioner for Iraq with the power (as the Bosnian high commissioner has) to veto orders by the Iraqi executive and legislation from the Iraqi parliament—although at this late date, it seems dubious that the Iraqis would accept such an official, even if the United States were willing.

In addition, another reason (the word "excuse" may be more accurate) offered up by America's European and other allies is that they cannot, politically or legally, participate in an occupation that was not authorized by the United Nations. Washington's willingness to accept a UN-authorized high commissioner, as part of a new American approach to the United Nations that agreed to allow the Security Council (and/or the Secretary General) a real role in Iraq's reconstruction, would effectively remove that obstacle. It might be enough to persuade some governments to join the coalition, and might make it impossible for others not to do so. In the end, some countries might still balk, but because it is so important to secure as many additional allied contributions as possible, it is critical for the United States to be seen as going the extra mile to meet the conditions laid out by these various countries for their support, and for most of them, the insecurity and the meager UN role have been their principal complaints. It still may not work, but the Administration must be willing to try.

Another stumbling block to garnering greater support through the United Nations has been, once again, the security situation. After the bombing of the UN headquarters, the Secretary General has been largely uninterested in putting additional UN personnel into the country. This provides still another incentive to deal with the security situation quickly—either by ramping up U.S. forces in a short-term surge or by shifting to a true COIN strategy.

If the United States could improve the security within all or part of the country, this should make it easier to convince Secretary General Kofi Annan to send people to Iraq, which should make it easier to secure allied military commitments, which should then allow the security situation to improve in a virtuous cycle. And, historically, post-conflict reconstructions generally follow either a virtuous cycle (with each positive development reinforcing other positive developments, which in turn reinforce the original positive developments) or a vicious cycle in which failures and problems feed off of one another to make everything progressively worse. We need the United Nations' help to create a virtuous cycle in Iraq.

Obviously, securing that support is going to be difficult, but it is worth the effort at least to try. Therefore, the Administration should sit down with both the P-5 representatives, other Security Council members, and the Secretary General, and make clear that the United States is willing to allow a UN-designated special representative to take the lead in certain areas of economic and political development in return for the United Nations providing real resources and real leadership. Washington should specify areas where it would like greater assistance from the United Nations in the political, economic, and social spheres, discuss what assistance and resources the United Nations could provide, and even agree to allow them to take the lead if we are convinced that doing so will be helpful. All of this should be codified in a new Security Council resolution and the functions stipulated as responsibilities of the new high commissioner.

ENGAGING THE NEIGHBORS

At Sharm al-Shaykh in November, the Bush Administration took the first step toward greater regional participation by convening a conference of Iraq's neighbors to discuss their participation in reconstruction. This was an important step, but the conference was not able to produce meaningful contributions from the allies and so a great deal more needs to be done.

All of Iraq's neighbors have considerable influence with different groups inside the country—especially the most problematic groups that are looking to pursue extreme or unilateral courses that would undermine stability and unity and could help push the country into civil war. In addition, many of them have real resources that could be of value to the process of reconstruction. Consequently, the United States would do well to make a greater effort to engage them in the reconstruction effort. In particular, Iran's support is vital to the success of reconstruction, and Washington must find ways to restore the back-channel cooperation in which Washington and Tehran engaged to their mutual benefit during Operation Enduring Freedom.

The Administration should institutionalize a conference with representatives from the United States, the United Kingdom, Iraq, and all of Iraq's neighbors—conducted under the auspices of the United Nations. In this forum, the United States, Britain, and Iraq should all regularly brief the other members on key developments, short- and long-term plans, and key requirements. All of the neighbors are deeply unhappy about developments inside Iraq, and being more forthcoming with information would be a huge first step toward assuaging their fears. In addition, they should be encouraged to make suggestions regarding future developments in the country. It will be impossible to prevent them from doing so under any circumstances, they may actually have some good ideas, and the more the Americans and Iraqis can be seen as solicitous of their opinion, the better the United States will be in a position to secure their assistance in every sense of the word.

In return, the Administration and the Iraqis should make clear that we expect the neighbors to provide support to the reconstruction. The Iraqi people tend to strongly dislike all of their neighbors for one reason or another; thus, Washington should avoid requesting large numbers of troops from these countries if at all possible. However, it probably would be reasonable to ask for smaller numbers of personnel from Jordan, Saudi Arabia, and Kuwait to serve as translators in Iraq. Likewise, these three governments and the Syrians should be encouraged to lean on Sunni tribal leaders to end their support for the insurgency and instead back the reconstruction.

Similarly, the Iranians need to be encouraged to remain supportive of reconstruction. The Administration needs to reassure them both that the United States will succeed and that it will not use a stable new Iraq as a base for future operations against Iran. And the Administration needs to encourage Tehran to continue to encourage their various proxies in Iraq to continue to work peacefully in support of reconstruction, and not against it.

Although the Saudis are no longer awash in money, they can certainly come up with several hundred million, if not several billion dollars in aid to Iraq. Finally, we need to give the Turks an incentive to remain patient and allow the Iraqis to work out their own power-sharing arrangement.

Again, the Administration needs to accept the reality that Iraq's neighbors have the ability to meddle in Iraqi affairs and to make the course of reconstruction more difficult—very difficult, in the case of Iran. The United States has to give them an incentive to use that influence constructively, and to contribute far more than they already have. That means treating them as valued partners in the course of reconstruction, although it should not mean giving them veto power over any decision agreed to by the interim Iraqi government and the United States and United Kingdom.

CONCLUSIONS

All is not lost in Iraq. There is still considerable good in the country, but the macro-trends there are not pointing in the right direction. All of the many small victories there are slowly being swamped by the overarching problems of insecurity, poor economic performance, and the growth of the insurgency (especially among Iraq's Sunni tribal community). Moreover, the political process to which the United States signed on for the sake of putting an Iraqi face on reconstruction quickly is one fraught with dangers for the country's long-term political stability. Even if the current political process works in the short term, within a year or two the poor fit of that system with the realities of Iraq could create much larger problems than those that the United States is facing today. There are potential solutions for all of these problems, but they have grown to the extent that they will require some very difficult decisions by the Bush Administration—including reversing course on some of the principal themes of the reconstruction to date. If the Administration can recognize its mistakes and correct its policies, there is every reason to believe that Iraq can eventually be turned around, and no reason to believe that the American public will be unwilling to do what would be necessary to achieve that vital goal.

Tackling Tehran

Kenneth M. Pollack

During his initial term in office, President Bush paid little attention to Iran. True, there was considerable tacit cooperation between Washington and Tehran during the wars in Afghanistan and Iraq, where their mutual interests superseded other considerations. But throughout its first four years, the Bush Administration could not bring itself to decide on an approach to Iran—belligerent or benign—and then pursue it. Instead, the Administration formulated a series of ad hoc responses that did little more than push off the problem for another day.

It is hard to blame the Administration too much for doing so. Iran today poses a difficult challenge for the United States. On the one hand, Tehran is probably the leading state sponsor of terrorism in the world, and the United States has pledged itself to wage a war on terrorism. In addition, new revelations have raised the specter that Iran's aggressive, anti-American regime will have nuclear weapons within a decade, and possibly in only a few years. On the other hand, since the 1978 revolution, the clerical regime has shown itself willing to make enormous sacrifices to achieve its goals (although its goals often seem bizarre to others). Moreover, because of Iran's size and its many problems, few military options seem worth the inevitable price that the United States would have to pay to execute them. Thus, the threat from Iran, and especially from a nuclear-armed Iran, is too great to ignore, but not so great that Americans would be willing to bear any burden to preclude it. Iran is not an easy problem to solve.

However, the cause is not hopeless. There are still courses that the United States could adopt that would have a real prospect of accomplishing at least some of our most important goals regarding Iran. But the opportunities we have today to deal with Iran's nuclear program and support for terrorism will not last forever. Today, Tehran's policy direction is still not locked in. Today, Iran still requires considerable external assistance for its nuclear program. Today, America's European allies are more concerned about Iran than they have been for 20 years. Today, a great many of Iran's neighbors would gladly help us to prevent Tehran from crossing the nuclear threshold. Today, the world is still ready to work with the United States on security issues like Iran.

The Chink in Iran's Armor

From the outside, Iran seems highly willing to shrug off outside efforts to pressure it. The clerical regime has frequently shrugged off costs that would have made any other government blanch. Neither the destruction of the Iran-Iraq War nor the pressure from comprehensive U.S. sanctions appear to have made much of an impact. The regime's leaders have shown a remarkable resilience in the face of numerous foreign and domestic challenges, including emasculating the widely popular reform movement that threatened to topple them just eight years ago. The regime has often been able to rally popular support against a wide range of challenges, including the current American (and now European) efforts to curb Iran's nuclear program. Nor does international opprobrium appear to have slowed them by even a step.

Looks, however, can be deceiving. First, Iran has often been far more sensitive to international pressure than is generally acknowledged. Iran's losses during the war forced the mullahs to make peace with Iraq, even though Khomeini compared it to drinking poison. American trade sanctions have undermined Iran's rearmament and hamstrung its oil industry, prompting repeated demands from Tehran that they be lifted, even while Iranian officials insisted that the sanctions caused them no pain. The Iranians have gone to great lengths to avoid foreign censure, including most recently their efforts to placate the International Atomic Energy Agency (IAEA) so as to avoid having their case "referred to the Security Council"—an uncertain threat since the Chinese have warned that they will veto any sanctions against Iran, but potentially an important blow to Iran's reputation.

Of greatest importance, Iran's leadership is highly sensitive to pressure on its economy. The Iranian economy is the Achilles' heel of the regime. The economy continues to flounder in double-digit inflation coupled with double-digit unemployment—a problem likely to worsen as ever more young Iranians come of age while job creation remains constant at best. These economic problems are the single greatest threat to their rule;

discontent has been growing in direct response to the economy's slide. Most of Iran's leaders (including Supreme Leader Khamene'i, former President Rafsanjani, and other members of the hardline cabal) recognize that they must have trade, aid, and huge amounts of foreign investment if they are to dig themselves out of this hole.

For the moment, high oil prices have given a short-term boost to Iran's economy. This has allowed Tehran to breathe something of a sigh of relief, but Iran's technocrats are well aware that this temporary boost will have little impact on Iran's long-term needs. Iranian economic officials have publicly stated that Iran will need $20 billion in investment each year for at least the next five years if Iran is to meet the employment needs of its burgeoning population, while the Iranian national oil company estimates that the country needs $70 billion to refurbish Iran's decrepit oil infrastructure. Such numbers as these cannot possibly be made up by a temporary, marginal rise in oil prices; Iranian officials acknowledge that this kind of capital can only come from overseas, and only from the United States, Europe, and Japan. Consequently, the current high oil prices will further complicate any American policy toward Iran (because some Iranian leaders will invariably believe that this gives them a bit more breathing room) but will not fundamentally change Iran's position or requirements.

Iran's long-term economic problems create considerable leverage for the rest of the world. Iran needs expanded commercial ties to Europe and Japan and/or a full-scale rapprochement with the United States if it is going to do more than just continue to tread water (and it is unclear that even that would be enough to prevent the economy, and with it domestic unrest, from worsening). The promise of such ties could be a powerful inducement. By the same token, the Iranian leadership clearly worries that Europe and Japan would join the United States in imposing multi-lateral trade sanctions that would diminish or even deny them the economic benefits they crave. This, too, is a very promising source of leverage over Iran.

TRIPLE TRACK

Although there is some reason for optimism regarding our ability to influence Iranian decision-making, doing so will nonetheless be difficult and may fail altogether. Opportunities are not guarantees. Consequently, the United States would do well to adopt a multi-track approach to Iran, in which each track reinforces and backs up the other two. I have elsewhere developed one such an approach, which I call "Triple Track."[1]

There are a number of basic principles that lie behind Triple Track. An effective U.S. policy toward Iran must be flexible. Because of its fragmented political spectrum and the closed nature of its policymaking process (coupled with the considerable ignorance of many of its policymakers), Iran can be extremely unpredictable. Therefore, the United States must be positioned to react both to Tehran's positive and negative moves. This unpredictability, coupled with the long history of troubled relations between Washington and Tehran, also mean that no U.S. policy toward Iran has a high likelihood of success. Since the Iranian regime often axiomatically defines its interests as being the opposite of whatever the United States wants, since the present leaders seem determined to hew to their nuclear and terrorism policies, and since many of them are willing to watch their country suffer rather than change course, it will be very difficult to do so.

Consequently, any American policy toward Iran should have a series of fallback positions to ensure that Washington is never caught flat-footed by the failure of its primary strategy. A new policy toward Iran should incorporate a variety of different approaches toward the problems posed by Iran, to enable the United States to deal with both the range of problems, the range of potential opportunities available, and the range of different Iranian responses. Last, because even a policy that successfully meets all of these conditions still runs a high risk of failure, a new policy toward Iran must be fully consistent with broader American foreign policy goals and principles. If at some point in the future Iran crosses the nuclear threshold, rendering American policy a failure, the U.S. government will need to be able to say that it remained true to America's values and did not fatally compromise some other foreign policy concern in the name of a desperate gambit to derail Iran's nuclear program.

TRACK ONE: HOLD OPEN THE PROSPECT OF A COMPREHENSIVE SETTLEMENT

Because it is unlikely that the United States would be willing to mount an invasion short of a major Iranian provocation, and we lack the intelligence to have high confidence in an air campaign targeted at Iran's nuclear sites, our best hope is to convince the Iranians to disband their nuclear program and end their support for terrorism because it is in their best interest to do so.

The most efficient way that the United States could do this would be through a comprehensive settlement—often referred to as a "Grand Bargain." Since the Iran-Contra affair, American administrations have been trying to find a way to sit down with their Iranian counterparts and strike a deal to resolve all of the problems lying between the two countries. In essence, it would mean the United States trading off its various political and economic sanctions against Iran in return for Iran desisting from terrorism, violent opposition to the Middle

---

1 This discussion is essentially excerpted from my book *The Persian Puzzle: The Conflict Between Iran and America* (New York: Random House, 2004), especially pp. 400–416.

East peace process, and pursuit of nuclear weapons—and agreeing to means to verify that it was complying with those obligations.

The United States has nothing to lose by continuing to say that Washington is open to an authoritative dialogue with appropriate officials of the Iranian government regarding our various sources of conflict. If these differences could be resolved through negotiations, it would be infinitely better for both sides. It would be the fastest route to a settlement (although no one should be under the impression that bargaining with the Iranians is going to be quick, pleasant, or straightforward), the one Iran would be most likely to uphold, and the approach least injurious to other U.S. interests. A peaceful, cooperative resolution would therefore be highly desirable, and the United States should make clear that it remains open to such a deal.

The problem is that a comprehensive settlement is much more easily proposed than consummated. The long, painful history of American-Iranian relations—from the Mosaddeq coup to the hostage crisis, the American "tilt" toward Iraq, and Iranian terrorist attacks on the United States—have repeatedly prevented those desirous of a negotiated settlement from being able to even start such a process. In the late 1990s, the Clinton Administration successfully put that historical baggage behind it and, with strong support from both parties in Congress, made a dramatic effort to coax Iran to the bargaining table. Although the Clinton Administration demonstrated a seriousness and a willingness to address Iranian grievances that stunned many Iranians, in the end its initiative came to naught because the hardliners in Tehran simply would not sit down and negotiate with the Great Satan.

So far, anti-Americanism has proven too great an issue in Iranian political culture and Iranian domestic politics for the mullahs to agree to a comprehensive settlement. Thus, while demonstrating its willingness to engage in such a process, Washington should not base its Iran policy on the assumption that such a Grand Bargain is likely to be accepted by Iran.

If and when the Iranians finally set aside their visceral animosity toward the U.S. government and are ready to work out a comprehensive deal, the process itself is likely to be long and excruciating. On the U.S. side alone, there are over a dozen laws and executive orders imposing different sanctions on Iran. In addition, there are any number of other restrictions on interactions with Iran built into a range of federal regulations. The baggage from so many past unsuccessful efforts to engage Iran will also loom over the American side of the negotiations. The U.S. government will also have to decide how to handle the numerous court cases that have been brought by the victims of Iranian terrorism in U.S. courts, and have been awarded millions of dollars worth of damages from Iran by American judges, when the Iranians failed to contest these cases, believing them illegal and irrelevant and so losing them by default.

Looking at the Iranian side, the Islamic Republic has typically tried to "negotiate" by demanding that the other side make a series of concessions up front, to which it then can choose whether and to what extent to respond. The Iranians might very well start with the same approach and it may take a long time to convince them that that is not a negotiation. Part of the process will also require the Iranian leadership to confront some truths that they have misrepresented to their people, if not themselves. In particular, Iranian leaders frequently claim that the remaining Iranian assets frozen by the United States amount to something in the neighborhood of $30–40 billion, when in actuality the real number is probably a fraction of that amount.

Of course, the United States will want guarantees that Iran is going to live up to its promises.

Paradoxically, the nuclear program may then be the easiest part to address. As then-National Security Adviser Rice once noted, "There is no mystery to voluntary disarmament. Countries that decide to disarm lead inspectors to weapons and production sites, answer questions before they are asked, state publicly and often the intention to disarm and urge their citizens to cooperate. The world knows from examples set by South Africa, Ukraine, and Kazakhstan what it looks like when a government decides that it will cooperatively give up its weapons of mass destruction. The critical common elements of these efforts include a high-level political commitment to disarm, national initiatives to dismantle weapons programs, and full cooperation and transparency."[2] Libya can now be added to that list, and the United States should demand that Iran do the same: no games, no lies, no repeatedly revised declarations, no leading inspectors around the country by the nose, no harassing the inspectors—no Iraqi version of inspections.

Much harder would be verifying that Iran has ended its involvement in terrorism, and the related problem of its violent opposition to a Middle East peace. In truth, the United States is likely to have considerable intelligence indicating whether or not Iran has ended its support for terrorism, but very little that it would be able to use in a court of law (or more precisely, the court of world opinion)—which could well be necessary if the agreements are codified and Iran chooses to try to skirt the edges. Hizballah should be disarmed and turned into a civilian political party in Lebanon, but that likely would require Syria's blessing too, and Damascus is unlikely to give that except in the context of a Syrian-Israeli peace treaty. Intercepted arms from Tehran—or simply Iranian weapons turning up in the hands of Hamas, Palestinian Islamic Jihad, and other terrorist groups should be clear violations of the terms, but the Iranians can always procure weapons from third parties.

Ultimately, because it likely would prove impossible to handle Iranian support for terrorism through inspections or technology-control regimes or high-tech gadgets that sniff the air in the way it is possible to look for evidence of a nuclear program, determining that the Iranians have fully complied with this aspect of any agreement will require that a Grand Bargain with Iran have escape clauses. The United States will need to be in a position to pay out the benefits to Iran incrementally over a protracted period, and to have the process be reversible at Washington's discretion (which will make it even more unpalatable for Iran). To do otherwise, however, would be to run the risk that Iran would agree, collect its benefits up front, and then cheat on its obligations to end terrorism and stop opposing a Middle East peace with violence, knowing how difficult it would be for the United States to prove otherwise. Iran will have to recognize that ending its pursuit of nuclear weapons, terrorism, and violent opposition to a Middle East peace are not one-time affairs but perpetual commitments, and that if it does not live up to those obligations it will lose the benefits of the Grand Bargain.

In return for Iran agreeing to meet these conditions, the United States should be prepared to be fairly forthcoming. An American administration should be ready to lift all of the sanctions on Iran, both those imposed by executive order and those imposed by legislation, as well as to remove all of our different regulations. Washington should be ready to conduct a universal settlement of all claims, including both private U.S. claims against Iran and Iranian claims against the United States, to determine the fate of Iran's frozen assets. The United States

---

2 Condoleezza Rice, "Why We Know Iraq is Lying," *The New York Times,* January 23, 2003.

should be willing to approve Iranian participation in international economic frameworks like the World Trade Organization (WTO), and support their applications for economic assistance from international financial institutions. If Iran fully abides by its obligations, the United States should even be willing to consider bilateral economic assistance to Iran. The United States should be willing to provide assurances that it will not attack Iran if it does not attack the United States or its allies, and should be willing to begin a broader process of regional security discussions, aimed eventually at producing a regional security framework and arms control agreements similar to the Commission for Security and Cooperation in Europe (CSCE) process to address Iran's legitimate security concerns.[3] Washington should be willing to pledge not to interfere in Iran's internal affairs, if Tehran wants it. The United States should also be ready to establish a contact group including all of Iraq's neighbors to provide a coordinating mechanism and a way for them to provide input into the process of Iraqi reconstruction, and Iran should be invited to participate to address its concerns about the future of Iraq.

A particularly sensitive question will be whether the United States should be willing to accept an Iranian nuclear energy program as part of the Grand Bargain. Although Iran sits on the second-largest natural gas reserves in the world, the Iranians can make a reasonable claim to nuclear energy. The shah wanted it, and other countries with significant petroleum reserves have still developed nuclear energy because this allows them to export more oil. Consequently, the United States should consider agreeing to allow Iran to purchase properly safeguarded light-water reactors in which the fissile material is supplied by another country (probably Russia), which also takes it back for reprocessing once it

is spent. It is still possible to make a nuclear weapon from the fissile material in a light-water reactor, but is harder to do so. It would likely become known if they were trying to do so, and therefore, Tehran would probably only take this step in the event of a crisis. Nevertheless, this risk could not be eliminated entirely, and so should reinforce Washington's determination to see that the terms of the Grand Bargain are only paid out incrementally over time to ensure that Iran always has an incentive to abide by its terms. Between the disarmament assurances that we will want, the difficulty of using properly safeguarded light-water reactors to supply a nuclear weapons program, and the ability to cut off the flow of benefits to Iran (and impose unilateral or even multilateral sanctions against Tehran if it is caught diverting materials to a weapons program), we should be as confident as it is possible to be that Iran will not be able to mount a clandestine program.

Of course, the bottom line remains that Iran has not shown itself ready to explore this option seriously for the past 20 years. As a result, the Grand Bargain cannot be the principal element of a new U.S. policy toward Iran during the Bush Administration's second term. At some point, the Iranians may be ready to sit down and work out a deal, but one has no idea whether that will happen tomorrow, ten years from tomorrow, or never. In the meantime, the nuclear clock is ticking and Iran continues to support terrorist groups. Thus, while there is no harm—and considerable benefit—in leaving the Grand Bargain on the table, making clear that it is America's preferred course of action, a new Iran policy will have to look to other strategies to deal with Iran's troublesome behavior until it finally can bring itself to sit down and work out its differences with the Great Satan.

---

3 For a fuller description of the utility and possible mechanics of such regional security frameworks see Kenneth M. Pollack, "Securing the Gulf," *Foreign Affairs* 82, no. 4 (July–August 2003).

Track Two: A True Carrot-and-Stick Approach

During the early 1990s, the United States pursued a policy of containment that relied essentially on punishment alone to try to coerce Iran into abandoning its nuclear program, support for terrorism, and violent opposition to the Middle East peace process. During that same period, Europe and Japan pursued a policy of engagement that relied on rewards alone to persuade Iran to do the same. Both approaches failed in this primary goal, although both enjoyed some modest success in secondary goals—European and Japanese companies did make a fair amount of money off trade with Iran, while the United States was able to constrain Iran's ability to rearm and pursue some of its most aggressive designs.

Both policies failed in their overall objectives because they were one-dimensional policies and neither side was willing to even entertain the idea of compromising with the other, which allowed the Iranians to play Europe and Japan off against the United States. As long as the Iranians could convince themselves that the Europeans and Japanese (and Russians and Chinese) would provide them with the aid and trade they needed without the same demands as the Americans, they felt they could withstand the pressure from the United States. Only a multilateral policy that combines the two approaches has any real chance of success in moving Iran in a positive direction on these various issues.

Convincing our European and Japanese allies (let alone the Russians and Chinese) to agree to sanctions against Iran in any form could be very difficult. To their credit, the Europeans have shown a greater willingness to threaten sanctions against Iran than ever before for Tehran's refusal to comply with the requests of the IAEA regarding its uranium enrichment and plutonium extraction activities. That is a step in the right direction, but

European capitals are still far from being willing to impose the kind of sanctions on Tehran that actually might persuade Iran to slow—let alone stop—its nuclear weapons programs. Moving the Iranians to that point during the next presidential term would require the Bush Administration to adopt two new approaches to the problem.

The first of these is that the United States must demonstrate a willingness to reward Iran, promptly and materially, for progress on the nuclear and terrorism issues. The most reasonable objections to America's policies that Europeans and Japanese raised in the 1990s were that the United States expected Iran to give up all of its problematic activities before Washington would consider making any changes to the sanctions, and that we were so obsessed with Iran's bad behavior that we were unwilling to even consider the possibility of rewarding Tehran for moving in a positive direction. The most moderate European and Japanese voices regularly stated that they would be willing to collaborate in a new policy toward Iran, but only if that policy included rewards for progressive actions in addition to punishments for recidivism. Moving Iran to give up its support for nuclear weapons and terrorism is going to be extraordinarily difficult. It is going to require both the push of negative incentives such as sanctions and the pull of positive inducements such as loans or liberalized trade.

The goal should be to present the Iranians with two different paths. If they choose to go down the path of confrontation—stubbornly clinging to their nuclear program, their support for terrorism, and their violent opposition to a Middle East peace—then at each step they will be hit with progressively more painful consequences. On the other hand, if they choose the path of cooperation —by giving up those same patterns of behavior— then at each step they would be rewarded with progressively more advantageous benefits.

Thus, the United States, Europe, Japan, and hopefully Russia and China should sit down and draw up a large list of "benchmarks," things that Iran could do that would be considered either confrontational or cooperative, and assign to each benchmark a corresponding positive or negative incentive proportionate to the step that it takes. This is simpler than it sounds, although the negotiations over exactly which benefits and penalties to apply for each benchmark undoubtedly will be long and painful. For instance, if Iran agreed to close down its uranium mines and turn over the extracted yellowcake to the IAEA, then the United States and its allies might agree not to block Iran's application to the WTO. On the other hand, if Iran brought the Natanz uranium enrichment facility on line, then the United States and its allies might agree to bar all imports from Iran. Likewise, at a lesser level, for every time that Iran tested a Shahab-series missile (including its engine), or that Hizballah attacked into Israel, the United States and its allies might declare a predesignated major Iranian economic project off limits to all of their corporations.

The benchmarks and incentives should also be set up to cover continuous activities (as opposed to one-time actions). Indeed, there is great value in locking in benchmark-incentive pairings for indefinite periods of time to reduce the risk that Iran might try to make a number of moves up front, collect the rewards, and then return to its previous patterns of behavior. For example, for as long as Iran agreed to forego uranium enrichment activities, the United States might agree to keep issuing waivers under the Iran and Libya Sanctions Act (ILSA).

The complete list of benchmarks and their corresponding incentives should be long. It should include both one-time and ongoing actions; it should address both positive and negative steps Iran could take on nuclear weapons, terrorism, and violent opposition to a Middle East peace; and it should include incentives covering the full range of political, economic, and military affairs. Moreover, both the positive and negative incentives must be graduated and accrue incrementally so that each time Iran takes a further step in either direction it is punished or rewarded immediately and proportionately.

It would be critical to lay out all of these different incentives up front, and there are three reasons for doing so.

- First, Iran needs to see both the whole series of penalties it will suffer if it takes the path of confrontation and the whole series of benefits it will gain if it takes the path of cooperation. There is a debate going on inside Iran on all of these issues, and it is critical to give those Iranians arguing for the path of cooperation all of the ammunition possible. Laying out very starkly the bright future that Iran could expect from choosing the route of cooperation compared to the grim future that it would face if it continued on the route of confrontation is probably the best that any outsider can do to influence that debate.

- Second, if presented with an imminent Iranian step in the wrong direction, many Europeans and Japanese will be sorely tempted to balk, as they have consistently done in the past. Only if the benchmarks and their consequences are clearly delineated well before Iran approaches them is it likely that our allies would agree to them and that the United States would be able to hold them to their commitments.

- Last, just as proponents of a Grand Bargain with Iran rightly argue that the Iranians will only be able to make concessions as part of a deal that includes the United States making counterbalancing concessions to them, so, too, is that true of forging a new Iran policy with our allies. The Europeans, Japanese, Russians, and Chinese have resisted even the hint of sanctions against Iran for over a decade; the only way that they might be willing to support any hypothetical sticks being used against Tehran is if they are presented as part of a comprehensive plan that also includes a corresponding set of carrots.

The Second Track should appeal to America's allies because it provides for sanctions only in the context of bad Iranian behavior—to which they will have agreed both that the behavior is bad and what the appropriate punishment should be. Moreover, it cushions the sanctions issue by coupling it with American agreement to reward Iran for good behavior, even small steps in the right direction—something that the United States has never agreed to do in the past. It leaves the actual imposition of sanctions or benefits in the hands of the Iranians. Since the benchmarks and their corresponding incentives will be defined beforehand, it is the Iranians who decide which course to take. If they choose the course of confrontation, it will be unmistakable that Iran is flouting the will of the international community and it will relieve the Europeans, the Japanese, and others of some of the need to consciously act to apply sanctions: in effect, the Iranians will be bringing the sanctions upon themselves, having been forewarned. At the same time, if Iran chooses cooperation, this too will be unmistakable. Americans will not be able to argue otherwise, and the Europeans will not have to try to persuade the United States to reward Iran since those thresholds will have already been set and the rewards should be automatic.

TRACK THREE: PREPARING FOR A NEW CONTAINMENT REGIME.

Although Iranian behavior over the past 25 years has demonstrated that Tehran does respond to negative (and occasionally positive) inducements, it has not always done so, nor has it always responded as expected. The mullahs in Tehran are capable of disregarding all kinds of damage to their country and passing up all kinds of opportunities, and they continue to exercise enough

sway over the population to be able to do so for the foreseeable future. Thus, while there is real reason to hope that a true carrot-and-stick approach as envisioned in the Second Track would move Iran in a progressive direction, the United States should not assume that it will. We must have a fallback option in the event that Iran remains unwilling to agree to a comprehensive settlement and stubbornly weathers a system of inducements and punishments designed to persuade it to become a more responsible member of the international community and discontinue its nuclear program.

Of necessity, that fallback option will have to be a revised version of containment. If the first and Second Tracks fail, the United States will be left with nothing but containment, one of the usual reasons that Washington has adopted containment in the past. Nevertheless, if at all possible, this containment regime should be somewhat different from the version employed in the early 1990s. It may be able to reap some benefits from even the partial successes of the Second Track, and it can be blended with elements of some of the other policy proposals—which are not feasible as stand-alone policies, but can be useful adjuncts to a policy of containment. Thus, while the United States pursues both the possibility of a Grand Bargain and creation of a multilateral incentive structure for Iran, Washington must also be preparing to mount a new containment system should both of those better options fail.

To a certain extent, the negative inducements of the Second Track (in other words, the "sticks") create the first elements of such a revised containment regime. In fact, they create the basis for a far more effective containment regime against Iran than the United States mounted unilaterally during the 1990s. That is one of the advantages of this approach—just as the positive inducements (the "carrots") of track 2 could become a path toward a Grand Bargain if the Iranians were ready for a more cooperative relationship, so the negative incentives lay the basis for a more robust, multilateral containment regime if Tehran persists in its preference for an aggressive, anti-status-quo policy. To a certain extent, as part of the Second Track's carrot-and-stick approach, the United States will be making a deal with Europe, Japan, and hopefully Russia and China as well. The Administration would agree to progressively reward Iran, including by lifting all of the sanctions, if Iran agrees to cease its problematic patterns of behavior, and it would agree to multilateral sanctions and a containment regime in the event that Iran refused to do so. If Iran did refuse to do so, it would find itself enmeshed in exactly the kind of multilateral sanctions regime that it successfully avoided before 1997.

The problem arises if America's allies also refuse to go along with Washington. Despite how self-evidently beneficial it would be for U.S. allies to join us in a structured carrot-and-stick approach to Tehran, Washington should not assume they will. All have repeatedly been willing to excuse egregious Iranian behavior and renege on commitments to hold Iran accountable for its actions. Thus, the Second Track might fail not because Iran is not responsive to the incentive structures, but because the Europeans, Japanese, Russians, and Chinese have refused to create such an incentive structure.

In this case, the key question the United States will face is whether to attempt to impose some of the various provisions of the Second Track unilaterally. Here, the provisions against Iran itself are essentially beside the point—the United States certainly could repeal the Clinton Administration's last gesture to Iran and again ban imports of Iranian carpets and foodstuffs—but these are mostly insignificant compared to its oil exports and its desire for American imports. The fact remains that the United States is basically doing everything it can to squeeze Iran through direct sanctions. The bigger question

would be whether the United States wanted to impose some of the sanctions envisioned in the Second Track against those countries helping Iran's nuclear program—in other words, more secondary sanctions like the ILSA. In this respect, the United States could announce that it will impose trade sanctions on foreign nations that provide Iran with nuclear-related materials—or that engage in the sale of plutonium or highly enriched uranium reactors or related technology in general. As another example, Washington could decide that unless the Europeans were willing to sign on to a multilateral effort aimed either specifically at Iran or against proliferators in general, it would no longer award any ILSA waivers (which would be appropriate given that the European Union's promise was to be more aggressive in combating both terrorism and proliferation). Other such secondary sanctions could certainly be envisioned.

Whether the United States should take this path is not a straightforward question and is almost impossible to answer beforehand. At such a hypothetical point, the United States would be playing a very weak hand against Iran. Throughout the 1990s, Washington attempted to change Iran's behavior through unilateral sanctions and was largely unsuccessful in doing so. At a future date, if confronted with the failure of the First and Second Tracks, with Iran getting ever closer to having a fully self-contained fuel cycle, it may prove even harder to do so. At that point, the Administration would need to ask how willing it is to damage America's relations with its primary trading partners to try to keep nuclear weapons out of Iran's hands.

The willingness of the Europeans, Japanese, Chinese, and Russians to take other actions against Iran will also play a role in such calculations. It is conceivable that they might take actions unilaterally—as they did with the mild but significant step of suspending trade expansion talks with Tehran in 2003—and in this case, secondary sanctions would likely be inappropriate. Finally, Iran's own internal dynamics should also weigh in on this decision. If Iran shows increasing signs of pragmatism (or if the reformists are somehow able to resurrect themselves), Washington may want to show forbearance in the expectation that a pragmatic Iran is more likely to be deterrable—and might even opt to discontinue its nuclear program on its own in hope of improving its international standing. On the other hand, while the willingness of the United States to take such steps unilaterally would undoubtedly further infuriate our allies, it could help persuade them that they should participate in the process envisioned in the Second Track—which would be more effective and consistent with their own policies—than face a trade war with the United States if we were forced to fall back on the Third Track without any allied support.

Beyond the question of sanctions, the United States could announce a policy of seizing any plane or ship believed to be carrying nuclear-related material to Tehran that American military forces are able to intercept. Such a policy might face some serious legal challenges, but would be consistent with the Bush Administration's own Proliferation Security Initiative, which proposed that the United States and its allies take precisely such steps to curb proliferation. The United States should also look for other ways to physically interdict nuclear-related shipments to Iran. Additionally, Washington should lay out a set of red lines for the use of force in hope of curbing some of Tehran's more egregious behavior—for instance, that the United States will hold Iran responsible for any act of terrorism committed by al-Qa'ida personnel in communication with the al-Qa'ida figures inside Iran.

In the military realm, the United States may need to reconfigure its forces in the Persian Gulf (which have mostly been focused on containing, then invading, and then rebuilding Iraq) to

better deal with Iran. This would include the need to interdict contraband being shipped to Iran, the ability to deal with renewed Iranian aggression against U.S. allies in the region, and forces in place to execute a counterproliferation option if the intelligence ever became available to do so. Indeed, as part of the Third Track, the United States should make a major intelligence effort—akin to the increase in U.S. efforts against al-Qa'ida after September 11—to gather information regarding Iran's nuclear program in the hope of developing a viable counterproliferation strike option. If the First and Second Tracks fail, then as part of a new containment regime as the final fallback position in the Third Track, the United States should take a much harder look at an air campaign against Iranian nuclear facilities and work much harder to try to make such an operation plausible. There are still likely to be strong diplomatic and military rationales against this strategy, but they may be less compelling if the United States has already failed either to entice the Iranians to bargain away their program, or to persuade U.S. allies to set up a multilateral incentive structure to convince Iran to do so.

Of course, one of the residual arguments against a counterproliferation strike is likely to be concern that Iran might retaliate by destabilizing Iraq. This raises another element of a third-track containment strategy, the need to keep Iran on the right side in Iraq. Here, it might be useful to pick up the idea of a contact group of neighboring states, specifically as a forum to give the Iranians a greater say in Iraq's reconstruction activities. If nothing else, it should reassure Tehran that the process of reconstruction envisioned by the United States and the new Iraqi authorities will not be inimical to Tehran's interests.

Finally, the United States should stick to its principles regarding Iran in all other respects. After the disgraceful rigging of the 2004 Majles elections, the relative quiet of the Bush Administration—which issued nothing but a perfunctory condemnation from the State Department spokesman—was shameful on Washington's part. It is likely that the Administration did so because the president's previous statements (from the inflammatory "Axis of Evil" to his much more moderate comments afterwards) only seemed to enrage the hardliners in Tehran. While this logic stems from good intentions, it flies in the face of U.S.-Iranian history. For the past 25 years the United States has not had any success trying to influence Iranian domestic politics. Typically, America's mere involvement has hurt whoever we have tried to help no matter how we tried to do so. Under those circumstances, it is vital that the United States maintain a consistent position advocating democratization, rule of law, religious tolerance, and respect for human rights in Iran. Remaining true to our convictions is critical to America's image in the world, which has been an important asset of American foreign policy over the past century. If the United States cannot help those in Iran it would like to see succeed, then at the very least Washington needs to remain true to its own values.

It is here that those who advocate a policy of regime change by pressing for a popular revolution illustrate a valuable kernel of truth. Throughout all of those years of the Cold War, it was important that the United States stood like a lighthouse on the other side of the Iron Curtain, reminding the peoples of Eastern Europe that there was a free world out there that believed in very different values and whose citizens enjoyed a much better life. As long as that beacon existed, it made Eastern Europeans—even if only in the deepest recesses of their subconscious—yearn for the end of communism. So, too, should the United States continue to play that role for Iran. The United States cannot help them directly because of the two countries' long, painful history and each side's psychological scars, but it can play an indirect role, as a reminder of what Iran might be if it were willing to move in a different direction.

Engaging Damascus

Flynt Leverett

Over the course of successive administrations, Democratic and Republican, the United States has defined an ambitious policy agenda toward Syria. This agenda has had both negative and positive dimensions.

On the negative side, Syria has long been engaged in behaviors that the United States considers threatening or offensive. These behaviors include virtually all of the post-Cold War "hot buttons": support for terrorism, development of weapons of mass destruction (WMD) capabilities, maintenance of a hegemonic position in Lebanon, and (until 1997) involvement in narcotics trafficking. This long record makes Syria, in many ways, a paradigmatic "rogue regime."

On the positive side, the United States has, under most recent administrations, recognized the centrality of Syria to Arab-Israeli peacemaking and the potential strategic gains from bringing Syria into the moderate Arab camp. As a result, the United States has never, at least until recently, treated Syria in the same manner as other Middle Eastern rogues, such as the Islamic Republic of Iran or Iraq under Saddam Hussein. Washington has consistently maintained normal diplomatic relations with Damascus. While the U.S. designation of Syria as a state sponsor of terrorism

brings the automatic imposition of specific U.S. sanctions on Damascus, Syria is the only state sponsor that has never been placed under comprehensive trade and economic sanctions. In addition, successive administrations have usually left Syria out of their more categorical statements about rogue regimes.

Indeed, during the 1990s, the Syrian track of the Middle East peace process provided a framework for sustained U.S. engagement with Damascus. In this approach, outstanding bilateral differences over terrorism and WMD were to be resolved in the context of a peace settlement between Israel and Syria.

ROOTS OF ESTRANGEMENT

During President George W. Bush's first term, the positive side of this agenda has atrophied dramatically and the negative side has become far more accentuated as a focus for American policy. To be fair, the traditional underpinnings for U.S. engagement disappeared in a six-month period in 2000—before Bush took office—with the collapse of the Syrian track at the summit between President Clinton and President Hafiz al-Asad in Geneva in April, the Israeli withdrawal from southern Lebanon the following month, Hafiz al-Asad's passing in June, and the outbreak of the al-Aqsa *intifada* in September. As a result of these events, President Bush came to office with no inherited operational framework for policy toward Syria.

In the post 9/11 environment, Syria's status as a state sponsor of terror pursuing WMD capabilities was bound to become a source of increasing friction between Washington and Damascus. Without an active and ongoing Syrian track, Damascus had lost an important part of its protection against American opprobrium.

Syria, under the new leadership of Bashar al-Asad, offered the United States intelligence cooperation against al-Qa'ida and related groups in the aftermath of the September 11 attacks, but did nothing to reverse its own terrorist ties. Syria added to the list of U.S. grievances against it by its continuing violations of UN sanctions imposed on Saddam's Iraq, by official Syrian complicity in the transfer of military and dual-use items to Iraq, and by Syrian facilitation of the movement of foreign fighters into Iraq during Operation Iraqi Freedom and afterwards.

As a result of these developments, Syria's standing in Washington declined significantly during the Bush Administration's first term in office. This decline was clearly reflected in the Administration's decision, during the second half of 2003, not to oppose passage of the Syria Accountability and Lebanese Sovereignty Restoration Act, which was passed by Congress and signed by President Bush that fall. As the president began his second term, the assassination of former Lebanese Prime Minister Rafiq Hariri in February 2005 sparked a further downward spiral in U.S.-Syrian relations, with Washington withdrawing its ambassador in Damascus for "urgent consultations."

A Policy Vacuum

Unfortunately, as Syrian-American relations deteriorated, President Bush and his senior advisers failed to develop a genuine policy toward Syria, if by "policy" one means an integrated series of public positions, diplomatic initiatives, and other measures (including, perhaps, the actual or threatened use of force, either overtly or covertly), all rooted in a strategy for persuading Syria to change its problematic behaviors and cooperate in the pursuit of U.S. goals. In a manner reminiscent of its first-term policy process regarding Iran, the Administration never resolved its internal differences over Syria policy, leaving it with an ineffective, "neither fish nor fowl" posture.

During its first term in office, the Administration was able to agree only on a laundry list of complaints about Syria's lack of cooperation with U.S. goals in Iraq, support for terror, and pursuit of WMD, which it has reiterated in largely unproductive diplomatic exchanges with Damascus. Although the Administration was able to coordinate effectively with France and other members of the United Nations Security Council to secure passage of United Nations Security Council Resolution 1559 in September 2004, the Bush team eschewed, for the most part, any serious or sustained effort to coordinate policy toward Syria with the European Union or other important international players.

As a result of these failures, the Bush Administration has had little success in getting Syria to modify its problematic behaviors or in cultivating a more constructive relationship with the Asad regime, despite letters and phone calls to Bashar from President Bush, personal meetings with Colin Powell during his tenure as Bush's secretary of state, and visits by other senior officials to Damascus.

As President Bush enters his second term, the United States still lacks a framework for dealing effectively with Syria. This policy vacuum is deleterious to U.S. interests, and needs to be corrected if the Administration is to formulate and sustain a more coherent strategy for the war on terror and for pursuing its agenda in the broader Middle East.

Strategic Underpinnings

What would optimal U.S. policy toward Syria look like?[1] Logically, one can identify four alternative strategic options for U.S. policy toward Syria: increasing sanctions and other forms of pressure, pursuing coercive regime change in Damascus, restarting the Syrian track of the Middle East peace process, and conditional engagement with the Asad regime outside of the peace process. Each of these strategies has its proponents among American foreign policy elites. Each also has its own historical record in U.S. policy, with particular reference either to Syria or to other cases.

Increasing Pressure

To the extent that current U.S. policy toward Syria can be said to reflect an underlying strategy, that strategy would seem to be one of trying to change Syrian behavior by increasing pressure on Damascus through additional unilateral sanctions and critical rhetoric. This is certainly the logic of the Syria Accountability and Lebanese Sovereignty Restoration Act (SALSA), which the Bush Administration began to implement in May 2004. More recently, the Administration has been taking preparatory steps to impose additional sanctions under SALSA—sanctions that would effectively shut down the operations of U.S. companies in Syria—and is considering imposing sanctions on Syria's financial sector under the Patriot Act. The withdrawal of the U.S.

ambassador in Damascus could also be considered, effectively, a sanction.

For their proponents, applying more sanctions to Syria has a symbolic value in conveying American displeasure with problematic Syrian behaviors. Unfortunately, there is little in the historical record to suggest that unilateral sanctions contribute significantly to the modification of those behaviors.

Imposing pressure on Syria through unilateral sanctions has a long and essentially unproductive record as a U.S. policy tool. Syria has been designated a state sponsor of terrorism since the state sponsors list was first published in 1979. Under U.S. law, state sponsor status carries with it the automatic imposition of several unilateral sanctions, including prohibitions on the sale or transfer of military items, restrictions on the transfer of dual-use items, a ban on U.S. assistance to designated governments, and mandatory U.S. opposition to the extension of support by international financial institutions to designated countries.

Twenty-five years of this approach do not seem to have affected Syrian behavior or strategic and tactical calculations appreciably. To argue that imposing additional unilateral sanctions, whether under the Syria Accountability Act or some other measure, will in itself be more effective in the future, one has to explain why a 25-year record of policy failure should not be taken as a predictor of the likely consequences of doing more of the same. The only circumstance under which sanctions might work to change a problematic regime's negative behavior is when the sanctions are multilateral in scope; unilateral sanctions usually only prompt the targeted state to diversify its trade partners. But in the Syrian case, European states, Japan, Russia, China, and other major players in the world economy are not

---

1 The following discussion is essentially excerpted from the author's *Inheriting Syria: Bashar's Trial by Fire* (Brookings Institution Press, forthcoming 2005), especially chapter 5.

prepared to join the United States in sanctioning the Asad regime over terrorism or WMD; it is not clear how far these actors (other than France) would go to press Damascus over Syrian hegemony in Lebanon.

COERCIVE REGIME CHANGE

In the context of the global war on terror, another approach that has emerged for dealing with problem states is the threatened or actual pursuit of coercive regime change. Coercive regime change can be pursued either through direct military action or through reliance on external opposition elements.

Since the September 11 attacks, coercive regime change through direct military action has become the centerpiece of the Bush Administration's approach to the war on terror. The United States carried out military campaigns for regime change in Afghanistan in 2001 and Iraq in 2003; obviously, in those cases, the use of force was an effective tool to topple problematic regimes. More recently, the Bush Administration has claimed that the perceived threat of being the next target for coercive regime change—a perception generated by U.S. military action to unseat Saddam Hussein in Iraq—drove Libyan leader Mu'ammar al-Qaddafi's decision to give up his WMD programs and renounce terrorism.

Neoconservative foreign policy advocates have long been interested in the possibility of pursuing coercive regime change in Syria. This interest antedates the September 11 attacks. Among those neoconservatives who entered the Bush Administration, there was considerable interest in determining whether Syria might not be the next target for U.S. military action following Operation Enduring Freedom in Afghanistan and Operation Iraqi Freedom. Although the Bush White House has not opted for pursuing regime change in Damascus, neoconservative advocates inside and outside the Administration continue to look at Syria as a prospective target.

Although the option of coercive regime change through direct military action offers the attraction of allowing the United States to seize the initiative toward a problematic state with policy instruments of unequaled effectiveness, it is not an all-purpose option. In some situations, as in Afghanistan under the Taliban, the use of force may be unavoidable and thus eminently justified on strategic and moral grounds. However, it is by no means clear that overthrowing the Asad regime is the only way to achieve U.S. policy goals toward Syria.

Moreover, ongoing commitments in Iraq make it doubtful that the United States has a serious option to launch "Operation Syrian Freedom" anytime soon. Notwithstanding its superpower status, the United States does not have the resources, either material or political, to resolve its differences with every problematic state around the world in this way in a time frame that is meaningful for the global war on terror. Logistically and operationally, the U.S. military has come under increasingly severe strain because of ongoing requirements in Afghanistan and Iraq. There are simply not enough military assets at U.S. disposal for an extended series of campaigns to topple troublesome regimes across the greater Middle East. Over time, as this state of affairs has become increasingly clear to regional observers, it has diminished whatever diplomatic utility the implicit threat of additional campaigns of coercive regime change might have had.

Politically, it is doubtful that the United States can maintain the international legitimacy of a global war on terror in the absence of strategic alternatives to coercive regime change. As noted in the introduction, the United States lost a substantial measure of support for the war on terror between Operation Enduring Freedom and Operation Iraqi Freedom. Further resort by the United States to coercive regime change in countries such as Syria, where other options are not widely perceived to be nonexistent or exhausted, would almost certainly reduce international support for the war on terror even more. Especially in the Arab and Muslim worlds, the risk of popular "blowback" against the United States would increase.

In the Syrian context, one would also have to consider the strong likelihood of post-conflict difficulties on a scale comparable to those confronted by U.S. and Coalition forces in Iraq. Syrian society is at least as complicated as Iraqi society, with similar tendencies toward fragmentation along ethnic and sectarian lines. Furthermore, the Iraq experience suggests that the U.S. government has a long way to go before Americans should be confident in its ability to anticipate the most likely difficulties in such challenging environments and plan effectively for post-conflict stabilization.

Given the prospective problems associated with pursuing coercive regime change in Syria through direct military action, some have suggested relying on external opposition elements to sweep away the Asad regime. A group of members of Congress are preparing a so-called Syria-Lebanon Liberation Act, modeled on the Iraq Liberation Act, to encourage such a strategy. There is, to be sure, a loose Syrian external opposition movement, consisting of exiled Muslim Brotherhood figures and secular opponents of the Asad regime in various European locales (mostly London and Paris). In 2002, a Syrian-American activist, Farid Ghadry, launched the Reform Party of Syria (RPS), putting the RPS forward as the core of a more vital external opposition to the Syrian regime.

Historically, however, a strategy of relying on an external opposition to bring about political change in authoritarian regimes has an unbroken record of failure as a guide for U.S. policy. The work of Miami-based Cuban exiles has done very little to improve the political situation in Cuba or the lives of ordinary Cubans. The exile strategy for regime change did not work in Iraq, either; direct foreign intervention was required to meet that goal. (Moreover, since the fall of Saddam's regime, the Coalition's over-reliance on returning exiles has arguably been one of the factors creating a risk of strategic failure for the United States in Iraq.)

Similarly, the Syrian expatriate opposition movement would seem to be an inadequate base for changing the political environment inside Syria. There is no evidence that exiled secular oppositionists have much of a following inside Syria; indigenous civil society activists eschew association with the exiles, preferring not to put their own standing within Syria in question. The one exception to this is the Kurdish Yakiti party, which has developed an affiliation with the Reform Party of Syria. However, given the risks of regional fallout from Kurdish separatist ambitions in a politically unsettled environment, the United States should be exceedingly cautious before opting to play the Kurdish card in Syria.

Even if an external opposition were somehow able to destabilize the Asad regime, the experience of Afghanistan and Iraq strongly suggests that it will not be easy to make a smooth transition to a new political order. Indeed, given the fractiousness inherent in Syrian society, the most likely political outcome in the near term would be chaos. The most likely alternative to emerge from that chaos would be a heavily Islamist state—hardly an advance for U.S. interests.

Restarting the Syrian Track

Among those inclined toward more constructive ways of dealing with Damascus, a number of analysts have focused on the importance of restarting a meaningful Syrian track of the Middle East peace process. Given the long experience of Israeli-Syrian negotiations in the 1990s, some have argued that renewal of the Syrian track is the best way for Washington to encourage the Asad regime to take a more conciliatory and cooperative posture toward U.S. concerns.[2] Others have suggested that, given the central importance of a return of the Golan Heights to Syrian control for both Hafiz and Bashar al-Asad, restarting negotiations toward that end is effectively the only way to engage the Asad regime.[3]

These arguments are not unsound. Certainly, the prospect of U.S. activism in the peace process was a key factor in winning Syrian support for the first Gulf War coalition. During the 1990s, the Syrian track was the framework for structuring the U.S.-Syrian relationship more broadly; it would be difficult to argue that the relationship was not in better shape in those years than today. Resumption of the Syrian track would allow a U.S. administration to put differences with Damascus over terrorism and WMD into a more politically manageable framework; it could also make it easier for the United States and Syria to cooperate on issues outside the Arab-Israeli arena, such as Iraq. Moreover, if a renewed Syrian track bore fruit, the benefits would be undeniable, above all for Israel. A treaty with Syria is essential for Israel to complete the "circle of peace," to use Shimon Peres's phrase, with its Arab neighbors. Peace with Syria would also eliminate Hizballah's terrorist threat to Israeli security and remove Iran's forward base in Lebanon.

Given all of these positives, if it is possible to restart peace negotiations between Israel and Syria, such a development would clearly serve U.S. interests. The Bush Administration, in its first term, paid far less attention to the Syrian track than it did to the Palestinian issue. The benefits of Israeli-Syrian peace for Israel and U.S. interests should prompt the Administration to overcome its first-term reluctance to lean forward on the possible resumption of the Syrian track. Nevertheless, the reality is that political conditions in both Syria and Israel would make it hard to bring the two parties back to the negotiating table any time soon.

On the Syrian side, it seems unlikely that Bashar would agree to a resumption of talks—or, if he started negotiations, to sustain them—without some sort of Israeli reaffirmation of Prime Minister Rabin's contingent commitment to full Israeli withdrawal from the Golan Heights if Israeli requirements for post-withdrawal security arrangements and normalization of bilateral relations were met (the now famous "deposit"). It is even more improbable that Bashar would conclude an agreement that did not meet his late father's conditions for an acceptable settlement—above all, the elder Asad's insistence on what could be plausibly portrayed as full Israeli withdrawal from the Golan Heights as the sine qua non for a peace agreement.

On the Israeli side, however, it is unlikely—given current political configurations in Israel and the tensions that have accumulated between Israel and Syria since 2000—that there will be an Israeli government willing to meet Syrian conditions for resuming and concluding peace talks in the near term. The chances that an Israeli government headed by Ariel Sharon would reaffirm the Rabin deposit as the basis for renewed negotiations with Syria seem low indeed. Over the last year, in particular, Sharon has shown no interest in the arguments of those in Israel's intelligence community and senior ranks of the IDF who favor such a course.

In his essay, Martin Indyk has constructed a brilliant scenario in which, after carrying out his Gaza disengagement initiative in 2005, Sharon opts for resuming negotiations with Syria to deflect pressure to repeat in the West Bank what

---

2 For example, this is the approach recommended in Steven Simon and Jonathan Stevenson, "The Road to Damascus," Foreign Affairs, vol. 83, no. 3 (May/June 2004).

3 See, for example, the testimony of Ambassador Richard Murphy to the Senate Foreign Relations Committee, October 30, 2003.

he had just completed in Gaza. While Sharon seems eminently capable of making that sort of complicated tactical calculation, there is no evidence to indicate that he would be willing to pay the price—chiefly, full withdrawal from the Golan—that Syria would require for a peace agreement.

Conditional Engagement

In light of the difficulties in restarting the Syrian track under present circumstances, the last strategic option for dealing with Syria is to engage Damascus without waiting for progress in the peace process. This would represent something of a historical departure in U.S. policy toward Syria, since the United States has yet to develop a framework for constructively engaging Damascus apart from the Syrian track.

What does a strategy of conditional engagement look like? Fundamentally, conditional engagement is a strategy for modifying the behavior of problematic regimes through hard-nosed, carrots-and-sticks engagement. The essence of conditional engagement is to contrast the benefits of cooperation with the likely costs of noncooperation—in other words, to tell rogue leaders what is in it for them if they change their behavior, and make sure they understand what will happen to them if they do not.

Although the United States has yet to try a strategy of conditional engagement with Syria, Washington has pursued this strategy successfully with other problematic regimes. Conditional engagement, started before the September 11 attacks, helped to get Sudan out of the terrorism business and on the road toward a settlement of its civil war; the country's regression into the horrors of Darfur does not fundamentally undercut the significance of these counterterrorism gains. Conditional engagement, started with British support during the Clinton Administration and picked up by the Bush Administration before the September 11 attacks, was also key to getting Libya to meet its obligations pursuant to the Lockerbie/Pan Am 103 case as defined in United Nations Security Council resolutions, removing the main barrier to U.S.-Libyan discussion of bilateral differences.[4]

In both these cases, the United States defined a clear *quid pro quo*—the lifting of multilateral sanctions—for specified positive changes in Sudanese and Libyan behavior regarding terrorism. The logic of conditional engagement also contributed to Libya's decision to abandon its WMD programs. Throughout the diplomatic dialogue with Tripoli over the Lockerbie case, U.S. representatives made clear that there would be no fundamental improvement of bilateral relations, including a lifting of U.S. sanctions, until U.S. concerns about Libyan WMD programs were addressed. On both Lockerbie and WMD issues, the United States employed a classic, carrots-and-sticks approach with Tripoli, making it clear that no progress was possible until U.S. concerns were definitively addressed, but also making it clear what benefits would accrue to Libya from cooperation. Washington is continuing this approach by declining to remove Libya from the list of state sponsors of terrorism until Tripoli has institutionalized a counter-terrorism dialogue with the United States and has satisfactorily addressed questions regarding its alleged involvement in a plot to assassinate Saudi Crown Prince Abdallah.

Unfortunately, the Bush Administration was unwilling, during its first term in office, to extend this approach to other state sponsors of terror, such as Syria, in the post-9/11 environment. In fact, the Administration decided soon after

---

4 On this point, see Flynt Leverett, "Why Libya Gave Up the Bomb," *The New York Times,* January 23, 2004 and Martin Indyk, "The Iraq war did not force Gaddafi's hand," *The Financial Times,* March 9, 2004.

September 11, 2001 that, as a matter of policy, it would not offer or define potential carrots for inducing state sponsors to change their problematic behaviors.

Would such a strategy work with regard to Syria, as it has worked to move Sudan in a positive direction on terrorism and to induce Libya to meet its international obligations in the Pan Am 103 case and renounce WMD? Or is Syria more analogous to Afghanistan under the Taliban or Saddam Hussein's Iraq—an irredeemable regime, incapable of modifying its behavior, regardless of the incentives and disincentives put in front of it? The answers to these questions lie in an assessment of Bashar al-Asad as a national leader.

Based on an analysis of Bashar's background, his views on reform, and his handling of domestic and foreign policy issues since assuming the presidency, it would seem that the Syrian president is, for U.S. purposes, "engageable."[5] On the positive side of the ledger, Bashar has demonstrated some reformist impulses. He is not an ideological fanatic like Mullah Muhammad Omar or thuggishly violent like Saddam Hussein. Bashar has made it clear that Syria needs to modernize, but he does not have a fully elaborated vision for reform and lacks the technocratic capacity to develop such a vision.

He has also made clear his view that Syria's long-term interests would be served by better relations with the United States—in part because of his need for external assistance and support to push reform at home. Bashar has frequently expressed to American and other foreign visitors his interest in an authoritative dialogue with the United States, something that has not been available to him with the Bush Administration. Bashar envisions, in this kind of dialogue, that both sides would put their various concerns on the table and would negotiate to put together a strategic "package." When asked what he would put on the table for Syria, Bashar notes three items: a return of the Golan Heights, a constructive relationship with whatever post-Saddam political structure emerges in Iraq, and a robust bilateral relationship with the United States to help him obtain the expertise and other resources he needs to advance Syria's internal reform.[6]

On the negative side of the ledger, Bashar's reformist impulses have been constrained by a strategically autistic but still powerful Old Guard and by the imperative to be perceived as keeping faith with his father's legacy. Bashar can fall into strident Ba'thist, anti-American rhetoric, and he is still trying to follow and adapt the strategic "script" he received from his father. But this script affords an opportunity for engaging Bashar, as well as putting limits on his flexibility; the script acknowledges the desirability for Syria of a better relationship with the United States while making a strategic breakthrough dependent on meeting conditions rooted in the tensions of Syrian domestic politics.

What all of this suggests is that Bashar could be a suitable subject for diplomatic engagement if engagement provides him with a clear road map to the desired goal and empowers him to move in that direction. To engage Bashar successfully, it is not enough to complain about problematic Syrian behaviors: U.S. diplomats have been doing that for 25 years, since Syria was first sanctioned as a state sponsor of terror. Instead, the United States must give Bashar explicit and specific targets for reversing problematic behaviors. And engagement must be backed by a set of policy tools that would impose costs for continued non-compliance with U.S. requirements but also promise significant benefits in

---

5 See, especially, chapters 3 and 4 of Leverett, *Inheriting Syria.*
6 Interview with the author, January 17, 2004.

the event of cooperation—in other words, carrots and sticks. In this way, Bashar can be empowered to set aside the preferences of the Old Guard.

But is it possible to engage Bashar outside a renewed Syrian track? Again, the answer would seem to be a qualified "yes." In early 2004, when asked whether it would be possible to "bracket" the issue of the Golan Heights to avoid having the possibilities for improved U.S.-Syrian ties held hostage to a peace process that is not likely to be very active in the near term, Bashar replied in the affirmative. With regard to the Golan's return, Bashar said, "we don't need our land back tomorrow or next week"; Syrians know that "it will come back to us" eventually. All that Bashar needed from Washington on the peace process to be able to work on other parts of a U.S.-Syrian strategic package is, by his own statement, "some words, some rhetoric."

Putting Together a Package

It is very much in the interest of the United States to explore this kind of strategic package with Syria, rooting such exploration in the logic of conditional engagement. To do this, the United States will need to sort out its priorities among its various policy objectives toward Syria. The furor surrounding Hariri's assassination has made such instrumental calculation more challenging, but no less necessary. Given the ongoing U.S. commitment to post-conflict stabilization in Iraq and the precedence of the global war on terror for America's post-9/11 foreign policy, it would seem that eliciting Syrian cooperation with U.S. goals in Iraq and getting Syria out of the terrorism business should be the top priorities. U.S. policymakers should link the ending of Syria's involvement in terrorism with initiatives to strengthen Bashar's position and his capacity to undertake internal reforms.

Other U.S. policy objectives, are either less pressing in the current environment or less immediately achievable in a manner supportive of the broad range of U.S. goals in the region. With regard to the WMD problem, for example, the solution is inevitably bound up with the achievement of Israeli-Syrian peace. It is also unlikely that the problem of Syria's standing in Lebanon will be resolved on a strictly bilateral U.S.-Syrian basis. This issue is more likely to be resolved through a process of negotiation between Syria and various power centers in Lebanon, almost certainly mediated by regional and international actors; complete resolution will only be achieved over time. The retrenchment of Syrian hegemony in Lebanon will also need to be implemented carefully to avoid a reemergence of sectarian conflict and violence. Prime Minister Sharon's national security advisor, Giora Eiland, recently echoed longstanding Israeli concerns that an overly precipitous Syrian withdrawal from Lebanon would pose a threat to Israeli security.[7] The most that the Bush Administration is likely to be able to achieve on the issue in the near term is, perhaps, a redeployment of Syrian troops to the Biqa'a (as called for in the Ta'if Accord) or the public promulgation by the Syrian and Lebanese governments of a tentative timetable for Syrian troop withdrawals.

Iraq

In Iraq, the United States and a new Iraqi government would benefit from sustained and more far-reaching coordination with Syria on problems of border security; in the longer run, a post-Saddam political order would acquire greater perceived legitimacy among Iraqis and regionally as a result of Syrian endorsement. To win greater Syrian cooperation with these U.S. goals, it is important to offer prospective accommodation of Syria's legitimate interests in post-Saddam Iraq, if Damascus helped the United

---

7 Nayla Assaf, "Israel report lauds Syrian presence in Lebanon: Argues withdrawal strengthens Hizbullah," *Daily Star*, December 2, 2004.

States and other international and regional partners tackle the security and political problems there.

To be maximally effective, accommodation of legitimate Syrian interests in Iraq should have both economic and strategic components. In the economic sphere, appropriate "carrots" to induce greater Syrian cooperation could include facilitation of Syrian-Iraqi trade and Syrian participation in Iraqi reconstruction. In the strategic sphere, Washington should indicate openness to dialogue with Damascus on Syria's diplomatic and political interests in Iraq. Such a dialogue could be launched under the rubric of a regional contact group for Iraq, but could then be taken into a freestanding bilateral channel. The multilateral conference on Iraq's future held in Sharm al-Shaykh in November 2004 could in theory serve as the starting point for establishing a contact group framework for Iraq, but it is not clear how assiduously the Bush Administration will follow up on the meeting. Alternatively, the United States could simply start a bilateral dialogue on Iraq with Damascus.

To be sure, within the Bush Administration, the State Department has been relatively forward-leaning in pushing for some kind of dialogue with Damascus regarding Iraq. But the idea has been resisted by harder-line elements in the interagency process, and the Syrians have yet to receive a clear signal from the Administration as to what they could expect in return for greater cooperation with U.S. goals in Iraq.

In looking at options for the Administration's second term, the possibility of an incipient strategic dialogue with the United States would be attractive to the Asad regime. The Asad regime has a longstanding and chronic fear of regional marginalization. Following the 1991 Persian Gulf War, Syria's principal forum for having its regional interests considered by the United States was the Syrian track of the Middle East peace process. In the aftermath of Saddam's overthrow, U.S. willingness to begin talking with Bashar about Syria's regional interests, with an initial focus on Iraq, would be an appropriate "carrot" for improving Syrian behavior. Among other things, it would allow Bashar to demonstrate to other powerful players in the regime that Syrian interests were better served by cooperation with the United States than by continued resistance to U.S. objectives. Over time, as Syrian behavior improved, a U.S.-Syrian strategic dialogue could be broadened to encompass other subjects of mutual interest, reinforcing this positive dynamic.

Of course, for a conditional engagement strategy to be complete, it must have sticks as well as carrots. And, in the case of Syria, the sticks probably need to go beyond the withholding of potential carrots to include the imposition of negative consequences. If Syria were not willing to increase and sustain its cooperation with U.S. objectives in Iraq, the most suitable negative consequence for the United States to impose would be to declare publicy its intention to send its military forces into Syrian territory at will in pursuit of insurgent cadres and to announce publicly each time it had done so.

Terrorism

In the context of the post-9/11 war on terror, getting Damascus out of the terrorism business is perhaps the most important near-to-medium-term U.S. policy objective toward Syria. Currently, Syria's status as a state sponsor of terror is the single biggest impediment to any sustained improvement in U.S.-Syrian relations.

In light of these considerations, the United States should adopt a new approach to managing Syria's designation as a state sponsor of terrorism. In the 1990s, the United States made Syria's removal from the state sponsors list contingent on a peace treaty with Israel that never came. In the present environment, it should now tie removal to changes in Syria's relations with terrorists. Specifically, the United States should indicate it would be prepared to take Syria off the state sponsors list, provided the Asad regime expelled terrorists from its territory, renewed counterterrorist cooperation with the United States against al-Qa'ida, and broadened that cooperation to include rolling back Syria's own terrorist links. Many readers may assume that this is already U.S. policy, and at least some U.S. diplomats will suggest that it is. But the fact of the matter is that the United States has never made such an offer to the Asad regime. Indeed, during the Clinton Administration, the policy was that Syria would get off the state sponsors list only in the context of a peace agreement with Israel. And, since the Bush Administration has been in office, it has declined to offer the Syrians the kind of "road map" for getting off the list advocated here.

Again, sticks need to accompany the carrots. On the terrorism issue, the United States should indicate that, in its view, the old rules of the game covering Syria's ties to terrorist groups and paramilitary proxies no longer apply. That means, first of all, that Syria cannot rely on Washington to restrain Israeli responses to terrorist provocations in quite the same way as in the past. While the United States clearly does not want to see escalating conflict along Israel's northern border or Israeli reoccupation of southern Lebanon, it may have a more tolerant posture toward Israeli retaliatory strikes against not only Syrian targets in Lebanon but also targets inside Syria. The international non-response to Israeli air strikes inside Syria in November 2003 provides something of a precedent that the United States could build on in making its diplomatic representations to Damascus.

As the United States defines a new approach to handling Syria's status as a state sponsor of terrorism, Syria's prospective removal from the state sponsors list should be tied explicitly to initiatives to strengthen Bashar's capacity for undertaking significant internal reform. It should be made clear to Damascus that taking Syria off the list would allow American economic aid to flow to the country for the first time in decades and substantially increase assistance from international financial institutions. Even though Syria's delisting as a state sponsor would be offered as a *quid pro quo* for Damascus effectively getting out of the terrorism business, the resulting opportunities to encourage significant internal reform would make this a win-win proposition for U.S. policy.

Linking Syria's delisting as a state sponsor of terror with measures to bolster Bashar's standing to carry out more sweeping internal changes would give a more strategic cast to the notion of promoting reform in Middle Eastern states as part of the war on terror. The Bush Administration has defined the promotion of fundamental political and economic transformation in the Middle East as a vital strategic objective in the war on terror, but it has not defined a high-level strategy for pursuing this objective. The lack of a strategy for promoting internal reform is particularly true with regard to states such as Iran and Syria, with which the United States has strained bilateral relations. The Administration has proposed a pair of initiatives—the Middle East Partnership Initiative (MEPI) and the Middle East Trade Initiative (METI)—to encourage transformation within and among regional states. Neither will apply in a substantial way to problem states like Syria. MEPI is essentially a compilation of already existing democracy-promotion and social reform programs; its funds cannot be spent in problem states like Syria. METI, too, is aimed almost entirely at states with which the United States already has some kind of strategic cooperation or, at least, a positive bilateral relationship; state sponsors of terror like Iran and Syria are deliberately excluded.

To lend further support to Syrian reform efforts,

the United States should modify other aspects of its current policy to strengthen Bashar's hand against those inside Syria resisting positive change. History would suggest that refusing to engage with either the Syrian regime or civil-society actors through provision of official assistance is counterproductive to the goal of encouraging greater openness, economic reform, and political liberalization. A strategy of simultaneously engaging authoritarian regimes in the early stages of reform and civil-society actors has had an impressive record of success, particularly in the former Soviet bloc and Latin America. This should be the model for U.S. policy toward Syria under Bashar al-Asad.

To that end, the United States should modify current provisions of its emerging initiatives for promoting economic and political reform in the greater Middle East to permit greater engagement with both regime and civil society in Syria. Two specific changes are in order. First, the United States should stop blocking Syria's application to begin the process of accession to the World Trade Organization. Like implementation of a prospective Association Agreement with the European Union, the WTO accession process holds the potential of helping Bashar overcome at least some of the deep-seated obstacles slowing or blocking economic reform in Syria. Second, the United States should permit official funds to flow to NGOs in Syria, even before diplomatic engagement might succeed in getting Syria out of the terrorism business. At present, the NGO movement in Syria is perhaps the most hopeful channel for promoting social and political reform in Syria, and merits U.S. support.

Once again, the logic of carrots and sticks should apply. As the United States steps up its support of NGOs in Syria, any effort by the regime in Damascus to constrain the activities of these groups should be the occasion for formal diplomatic protest and perhaps even public criticism along the lines of the Bush Administration's posture regarding Egypt's detention of Saad Eddin Ibrahim in 2001–2002.

COMPLETING THE "CIRCLE OF PEACE"

As noted, other issues of concern to the United States—including Syria's pursuit of WMD and its ongoing occupation of Lebanon—are likely to be resolved only in the context of an Israeli-Syrian peace settlement. Given an assessment that a resumption of Israeli-Syrian peace talks is not likely in the near term, what should the United States do to manage these issues in the meantime?

As noted above, Bashar believes that he needs rhetorical cover from the United States regarding the Syrian track in order to move ahead and deal with Washington over other issues. As it is in the U.S. interest to explore a strategic package with Syria focusing on Iraq, terrorism, and the promotion of internal reform, it is also in the U.S. interest to offer such rhetorical cover, consistent with Washington's traditional role as sponsor of the peace process and with Israeli security interests.

There are two possible vehicles for providing Bashar cover for moving ahead on other issues in the absence of concrete progress on the return of the Golan Heights to Syrian control. First, the United States could indicate bilaterally to Damascus that it understands Syrian requirements for peace with Israel, and is open to working for an agreement meeting those requirements, as long as Israeli requirements for a settlement are also addressed. Alternatively, the United States could endorse more fully than it has so far the 2002 Arab League peace initiative, while noting that final boundaries between Israel and its Arab neighbors remained, ultimately, subjects for negotiation among the parties.[8] Such a posture

---

8 In this context, the United States should note that a "just and agreed" resolution to the refugee issue, as described in the 2002 Beirut summit declaration, should and would not mean an outcome that threatened Israel's Jewish character.

would, among other things, convey to Damascus that the United States understands an Israeli-Syrian agreement returning significantly less than all of the Golan Heights to Syrian control is not diplomatically plausible for Syria and the other Arab states. The two approaches, of course, are not mutually exclusive.

Would either or both of these approaches provide sufficient cover for Bashar to respond constructively to a U.S. strategy of conditional engagement? The chances would seem relatively good. As the discussion in Martin Indyk's essay suggests, the strategic value of Syria's ties to anti-Israeli terrorist groups has already declined, in ways that Bashar appears to appreciate. In that context, U.S. adoption of either or both of the positions described above with regard to the fundamental parameters for a renewed Syrian track would send an important signal to Bashar that giving up Syria's terrorist "cards" would not compromise his chances of an acceptable peace agreement down the road. In fact, such a U.S. position would allow Bashar to argue within the regime and publicly that cooperation with Washington on terrorism would bring Syria closer to its goal of regaining the Golan.

In return for such an understanding with the United States, Bashar should be asked to acknowledge, at least privately, that questions regarding Syria's WMD and its presence in Lebanon would need to be addressed definitively.

These, then, are the elements of a U.S.-Syrian strategic package rooted in a realistic assessment of on-the-ground political realities in Syria. By working toward such a package, the United States could improve its situation in Iraq, make appreciable gains in the war on terror, and accelerate the pace of internal reform in Syria. In the process, Washington could also lay the foundations for an eventual Israeli-Syrian peace and establish predicate conditions for dealing with Syria's WMD programs and occupation of Lebanon. It would be truly disappointing, at a time when the U.S. position is under severe challenge in the Middle East, if the American body politic were unable to muster the wherewithal for proceeding with policies so manifestly in the U.S. interest.

Reengaging Riyadh

Flynt Leverett

The sixty-year strategic partnership between the United States and the Kingdom of Saudi Arabia has been one of the foundational pillars of America's Middle East policy for a dozen presidential administrations of both parties. At present, though, that partnership is in trouble, as a consequence of developments on both sides of the relationship during the Bush Administration's first term. If President Bush is not able to restore the U.S.-Saudi partnership, the chances for a substantial failure of American Middle East policy during his second term will increase significantly.

THE IMPORTANCE OF INTERESTS

Frequently described as resting on an "oil for security" bargain, the U.S.-Saudi relationship in fact reflects the overlap of a wide range of the two sides' strategic interests.[1] During the Cold War, the Saudi leadership perceived a dangerous Soviet military threat, and were deeply opposed to the revolutionary ethos of communist doctrine and the radicalism of Moscow's regional allies. Proclaiming an irreconcilable tension between atheist Marxism and Islam, the Saudi regime was for decades an important ally for the United States in its regional and global competition with the Soviet Union.

As a result, well before Anwar Sadat brought Egypt out of the Soviet orbit and into peaceful coexistence with Israel, Saudi Arabia was an essential platform for American efforts to develop a camp of moderate Arab states interested in regional stability and positively disposed toward U.S. strategic goals. In the 1960s and 1970s, Saudi leaders used their influence and (particularly after 1973) money to consolidate pro-Western regimes in the region and deradicalize Soviet clients (including Egypt). In the 1970s and 1980s, Saudi Arabia contributed billions to various anti-communist governments and political movements around the world to support American foreign policy goals. During the Reagan Administration's "second Cold War," the Saudis provided critical assistance to U.S. efforts to support Afghan *mujahidin* resisting the Soviet invasion of Afghanistan.

In the post-Cold War period, the United States and Saudi Arabia developed, in some respects, an

---

1 For a historical overview of U.S.-Saudi relations, see Thomas Lippman, *Inside the Mirage: America's Fragile Partnership with Saudi Arabia* (Westview, 2004).

even closer strategic partnership. Motivated by threats from expansionist neighbors and radical Islamist ideologies, Saudi leaders took steps that gave the kingdom a major role in America's capabilities to project power into the strategically vital Persian Gulf and were quietly supportive of U.S. efforts to foster a more stable region. Following Iraq's invasion of Kuwait in 1990, the House of Saud "bit the bullet" and invited U.S. and other foreign forces to defend the kingdom. Despite serious internal discontent with these deployments of "infidel" troops on Saudi territory, the regime remained steadfast in its cooperation with the United States, which was essential to the success of the coalition campaign to dislodge Saddam Hussein from Kuwait and restore the rule of the pro-American al-Sabah family.

Throughout the 1990s, forward basing in the kingdom was an important part of America's military posture in the Gulf, enabling Washington to enforce containment of Iraq and deter possible aggression by Iran. Almost as significantly, the Saudi Government contributed $100 million to an international fund for Palestinian development created after the signing of the Israeli-Palestinian interim accord in 1994, quietly demonstrating its willingness to support a peaceful settlement to the Israeli-Palestinian conflict.

And of course, Saudi Arabia has long occupied a uniquely dominant role among the world's oil producers. More than 60 percent of proven oil reserves in the world are clustered in the Persian Gulf. On its own, Saudi Arabia accounts for 25 percent of global reserves, dwarfing the reserve capacity of any of its neighbors.[2] Saudi leaders have frequently used the "swing producer" status afforded the kingdom by its reserves to moderate spikes in the world market price for oil, to the benefit of the United States and other Western economies.

THE DANGERS OF INATTENTION

As will be argued below, in the aftermath of the 9/11 attacks, the justification for collaboration between the United States and Saudi Arabia is every bit as compelling as before. But notwithstanding the seriousness of the interests at stake—and contrary to expectations in some quarters, given his family's perceived closeness to the Saudi royal family—President Bush was not a particularly assiduous manager of the U.S.-Saudi partnership during his first four years in the White House, for reasons rooted in domestic politics and divisions within his Administration.

There has been a perceptible anti-Saudi backlash within the American body politic since the September 11 attacks, with polls indicating that fewer than one-third of Americans have a favorable opinion of Saudi Arabia. The fact that fifteen of the nineteen 9/11 hijackers were of Saudi origin prompted a more thoroughgoing debate over the U.S. relationship with the kingdom than at any time since the 1973-4 Arab oil embargo. On a host of issues—including the war on terror and energy prices—a growing chorus of voices argues that the United States has not been getting an acceptable return from its longstanding commitment to Saudi security.

The 9/11 Commission concluded that no foreign government, including that of Saudi Arabia, had helped to fund the September 11 attacks. Nevertheless, Senator Bob Graham, former chairman of the Senate Select Committee on Intelligence who co-chaired a congressional investigation into the September 11 attacks, has argued that the 9/11 hijackers were actively supported by elements of the Saudi government. In July 2003, 191 members of the House of Representatives supported a bill to add Saudi

---

2 By comparison, Iraq follows with 11 percent of the world's proven reserves, while Kuwait, the United Arab Emirates, and Iran all have 9 percent each.

Arabia to the official State Department list of state sponsors of terrorism. This year, versions of a so-called "Saudi Accountability Act" (named after the Syria Accountability Act) were introduced in both the House and the Senate. Perceptions that Saudi Arabia was not doing enough to hold down rising oil prices provided fodder for politically popular criticisms of the kingdom by Democratic presidential candidates—including Democratic nominee John Kerry—during the 2004 election campaign.

As anti-Saudi sentiment has built up within the American body politic, the Bush Administration has not carried out any kind of fundamental review of the U.S. relationship with Saudi Arabia. The Administration has been divided between "realist" defenders of the relationship and "neoconservative" critics of Saudi behavior and practice; some neoconservatives question the wisdom of a strategic relationship based on an alliance with what they see as a corrupt, illegitimate, Taliban-like theocracy. As a result, there has not been a strong public defense of the relationship from the president or his closest advisers. In fact, there have been important opportunities for such a public defense which the Administration has, seemingly deliberately, let slide.

Constrained by these divisions among national security principals and facing a post-9/11 anti-Saudi backlash in the United States, President Bush seemingly could not decide on a clear course for U.S. policy toward the kingdom or how Saudi Arabia fit into his Administration's broader strategy for the region. As a result, he essentially neglected the substance of this critical bilateral relationship during his first term, notwithstanding the Bush family's longstanding ties to the Saudi establishment and the president's own high regard and solicitude for the kingdom's effective ruler, Crown Prince Abdallah.

This neglect came at a cost for the Administration's pursuit of the war on terror. Counter-terrorism cooperation after the September 11 attacks has been a highly controversial issue on both sides of the relationship. The Administration was able to effect what senior officials were willing to describe as significant improvements in Saudi intelligence sharing on terrorist targets and cooperation on stopping the flow of money to terrorist organizations from the kingdom only after the May 12, 2003 bomb attacks in Riyadh focused Saudi authorities on the terrorist threat within the kingdom's borders.

Saudi contributions to the Administration's major military undertakings also diminished significantly over the course of the president's first term. Saudi Arabia did not contribute troops to Operation Enduring Freedom; the United States ruled out participation of Saudi troops in Afghanistan because of the presence of foreign fighters of Saudi origin there. However, Saudi-based U.S. military aircraft did play an important role in the air campaign over Afghanistan. Saudi Arabia also did not contribute troops to Operation Iraqi Freedom, but did allow overflight for U.S. military aircraft during the Iraq war. Abdallah proposed creating a peacekeeping force drawn from Muslim countries not bordering Iraq for deployment there, but his plan was greeted with skepticism by the Administration and never implemented. In the aftermath of the Iraq war, U.S. military forces relocated out of the kingdom altogether.

Hard Times in Riyadh

The decline in U.S.-Saudi relations has taken place at a time of severe internal challenges for the kingdom and its rulers. It is no exaggeration to assert that Saudi Arabia is today going through a period of challenge unprecedented in its modern history as a nation-state. The challenge confronting the kingdom has at least three dimensions. First, Saudi leaders face urgent imperatives to reform, economically and politically. On the economic front, the basic facts have become familiar. The Saudi population displays the classic characteristics of a "youth bulge:" 46 percent of the population is 14 years of age or younger. Even if the current Saudi birth rate of more than 3 percent per year is cut dramatically, there will be a steady increase in the number of youths entering the job market each year for at least the next two decades, putting growing pressure on the economy's ability to employ them. But the Saudi economy is ill prepared to meet the challenge of absorbing a rapidly growing labor force. Thirty percent of young Saudi males are currently unemployed, and many more are under-employed, with no relief in sight. Most graduates of Saudi high schools and universities are not equipped to take the jobs that are available.

Rising oil prices over the last couple of years have not solved the problem of private-sector job creation in the Saudi economy, and almost certainly will not do so even if sustained for a considerable period. As the most recent report on the Saudi economy by the Saudi American Bank notes, more than a year and a half into the current oil boom, job generation is still "below the rate needed to create adequate new jobs for Saudis." Even if one assumes that the global energy market is entering a new historical phase characterized by elevated demand, in which Saudi oil production will average 8-10 million b/d at prices of $25–35 per barrel for the next several years (as compared to the previous 20 years in which Saudi production hovered around 6–8 million b/d at prices of $15–25 per barrel), the kingdom will have to undertake significant economic restructuring to boost the rate of private-sector job creation.

Saudi leaders are facing these imperatives to improve the kingdom's economic performance and reform the educational system during a period in which significant segments of the population are asking for more of a voice in political decision making. Crown Prince Abdallah received no fewer than five petitions in 2003 calling for substantial reform of the kingdom's political and social life, and a separate petition called for an end to discrimination against Saudi Shi'a—all this in a country in which such activities in the past have landed petitioners in jail.

Second, Saudi Arabia is going through a far-reaching internal discussion over the role of Wahhabi Islam in Saudi society. This debate is linked to the discussion of specific economic, political, and other policy reforms, but also encompasses some of the most potentially inflammatory issues in Saudi society, including the political and social standing of women and the appropriate status of Saudi Shi'a. This debate also plays out between defenders of the Saudi establishment and those who find the status quo insufficiently true to Islamic precepts and principles.

Third, against this backdrop of ongoing cultural, economic, political, and social challenges, Saudi Arabia is experiencing a sustained campaign of terrorist violence. This campaign emerged following the September 11 attacks; it escalated dramatically in the aftermath of the U.S. military campaign to unseat Saddam Hussein. To some degree, terrorist violence in the kingdom grows out of the various sets of internal challenges confronting the Saudi regime; at the same time, internal violence works to exacerbate these problems.

Declining relations with the United States since the September 11 attacks have complicated the task Saudi leaders face in managing their internal challenges. Saudi elites have begun to question whether the U.S. commitment to defend the kingdom remains as strong has it has been, and Saudi public opinion has grown ever more anti-American. In the face of mounting criticism of the kingdom in the United States, President Bush's less than vigorous public defense of the U.S.-Saudi relationship has been problematic for the Saudi leadership. In particular, the president's posture has increased Crown Prince Abdallah's vulnerability to criticism by other senior princes and strengthened resistance to his reform initiatives.

Abdallah believes that Saudi Arabia has not received sufficient credit in the United States for improvements in counterterrorism cooperation, including a more proactive posture toward terrorist financing. American visitors note that Abdallah continues to express a relatively positive assessment of President Bush, a view reflecting the crown prince's high regard for the president's father and a perception of man-to-man understanding with the president forged at the two leaders' April 2002 meeting in Crawford, Texas. Abdallah, however, also expresses his view that President Bush is ill-served by his advisers, and he has felt betrayed by several aspects of the president's Middle East policy, including:

- his neglect of the Palestinian issue (despite the president's personal commitment to Abdallah to deal seriously with it and in the face of Abdallah's efforts to support American engagement on the issue by offering his own peace initiative in 2002, which was endorsed by the Arab League);

- his high-profile reference, in the landmark 2003 speech on economic and political reform in the Middle East, to the sixty-year "mistake" of successive administrations in pursuing strategic cooperation with authoritarian Middle Eastern regimes; and

- his refusal—notwithstanding a special trip to Washington by Foreign Minister Prince Saud al-Faisal to appeal personally to President Bush in the Oval Office—to direct the Central Intelligence Agency to declassify the part of the joint congressional report on the September 11 attacks dealing with Saudi involvement, which would have permitted this section of the report to be released publicly.

Moreover, from a Saudi perspective, the Bush Administration's policies have contributed to the emergence of a disturbing internal security situation in Saudi Arabia. In particular, the forcible overthrow of a Sunni strongman in Baghdad followed by a chaotic U.S. occupation of Iraq with a still uncertain outcome tilted the balance between Sunni and Shi'a in the Persian Gulf region. Current trends in Iraq—which Saudi leaders see largely as the consequence of American ineptitude—are posing at least two ongoing problems for the Saudi regime.

Since the spring of 2003, the ongoing American occupation of Iraq has become a target for stepped-up attacks by "Binladenist" militants, operating alongside indigenous Iraqi insurgents. This has helped to inflame Sunni Islamist sentiment inside the kingdom. It also appears to have been an important catalytic event intensifying the shift of focus for Saudi militants and their supporters from jihad abroad to jihad in neighboring Iraq—and to jihad at home.

Sunni militant activity in Iraq also contributes to internal security difficulties inside the kingdom as militants of Saudi origin come home to continue their jihad. Senior Saudi officials acknowledge privately that they are at least as concerned about the flow of Binladenist personnel and supplies from Iraq into the kingdom as they are about the flow of money and people from the kingdom into Iraq. Indeed, supply lines to the kingdom's Sunni militants from the north may now pose as much of a problem as traditional lines of communication from Yemen in the south.

An additional problematic consequence of the Bush Administration's regional policies for Saudi Arabia's long-term stability is the impact of the Iraq war on Iran's relative standing as a regional player. In the aftermath of Saddam Hussein's overthrow, Iran is bound to emerge as a more powerful state in the regional balance.

The prospect of a nuclear-capable Iran under consolidated conservative leadership (with reformist President Khatami stepping down in 2005) represents a potential watershed in the Persian Gulf's balance of power. It may also represent a potential watershed in the political consciousness of the Shi'ite population in Saudi Arabia's oil-rich Eastern Province; the impact of this development could be exacerbated by the rise of a dominant Shi'ite majority in Iraq. The impact on Saudi Shi'a of an increase in Iran's regional power and assertiveness would also be exacerbated if a consolidated conservative leadership in Tehran decided once again to provide material support to disaffected Shi'a in the kingdom; such support was discountinued in the late 1990s as part of Khatami's "good neighbor" policy toward Saudi Arabia and other Gulf Arab states with significant Shi'ite minorities.

In light of these strategically dysfunctional features of the Bush Administration's policies (from a Saudi perspective), it should not be a cause for surprise in official Washington that the Saudi regime has begun to distance itself, in some ways, from the United States. While the United States had its own reasons for deciding to remove its military forces in Saudi Arabia, the drawdown of U.S. military personnel from the kingdom is also a manifestation of the Saudi regime's interest in a less proximate security relationship with Washington. Saudi interest in "hedging" the kingdom's strategic position is also evident in Riyadh's cultivation of China as a new and important customer for Saudi oil, a provider of consumer and manufactured goods to the Saudi market, and a prospective supplier of military hardware to the Saudi armed forces and security apparatus. Additionally, some Saudi officials indicate privately their appreciation of the potential leverage over American decision making that China derives from its position as a major holder of U.S. government securities.

The Need for Reengagement

In his second term, the President will not be able to achieve his near-to-medium-term objectives in prosecuting the war on terror, reconstructing Iraq, or containing Iran (either while an effort is being made to engage the Islamic Republic diplomatically or in the aftermath of a failed effort) without a more efficacious policy toward Saudi Arabia. Authors of several of the other essays have already identified arenas in which Saudi cooperation is critical to the achievement of U.S. policy goals.

- Saudi Arabia is, truly, "ground zero" in the war on terror. The Bush Administration cannot succeed in refocusing the war on "Binladenism," in the manner described by Shibley Telhami and James Steinberg, without the kingdom's full engagement.

- Martin Indyk has pointed out the importance of moderate Arab support to the emergence of a moderate post-Arafat Palestinian leadership. In that context, Saudi involvement is essential.

- As noted in Kenneth Pollack's analysis of Iraqi reconstruction, eliciting greater cooperation from Iraq's neighbors is likely to be critical to establishing workable arrangements for power sharing among the country's ethnic and sectarian communities and addressing the particular concerns of Iraqi Sunnis. Such cooperation almost certainly will not be forthcoming or effective without the cover of constructive Saudi participation.

Moreover, even though U.S. troops are gone from the kingdom, Saudi support is still needed to ensure that an ongoing U.S. military presence in other Gulf states remains politically sustainable. Saudi Arabia cannot simply become "flyover land" where the only thing the U.S. government wants is periodic overflight clearances for U.S. military aircraft. It must remain an active partner for the United States in providing security for the region.

Looking longer-term, Saudi Arabia remains key to achieving several important strategic objectives for the United States. Saudi Arabia is, in many respects, the "big enchilada" when it comes to promoting reform in the broader Middle East. The special place that Saudi Arabia holds, psychologically and symbolically, in the lives of Muslims worldwide cannot be underestimated. If the United States could work with the Saudi regime to encourage sustained economic reform and orderly political liberalization, the potential spillover effects elsewhere in the Arab and Muslim worlds would be enormous—arguably, greater than the effects of whatever positive outcome the United States might achieve in Iraq. Just as Saudi support is essential in the near-to-medium term to maintaining the current U.S. military presence in the Gulf, Saudi Arabia in the longer term must also be an integral part of whatever post-Saddam security structures are developed for the Gulf.

Thus, reinvigorating the U.S.-Saudi partnership is an indispensable part of a truly comprehensive Middle East policy in President Bush's second term. Reinvigorating the partnership, though, will require new approaches from the president and his foreign policy team. Above all, the Bush Administration will have to develop a strategic framework for its Saudi policy—a task that it avoided during the first term.

Beyond the importance of a more productive U.S.-Saudi relationship to the achievement of the Bush Administration's policy goals in the region, there is the increasingly daunting challenge of energy security. For the duration of President Bush's tenure and beyond, Saudi Arabia will remain the dominant swing producer for global oil markets, making the relationship with the kingdom the most important bilateral relationship for U.S. energy policy. Indeed, in coming years the oil-producing states of the Persian Gulf region are likely to become even more critical to the world's energy markets than they are now; within the Gulf region, Saudi Arabia will clearly continue to be the major player for oil production and export.

In late 2004, Saudi authorities announced plans to increase the kingdom's reserves by 77 percent through new discoveries and the increase of production in existing fields. Although that target may well be inflated, it is very difficult to construct a scenario in which Saudi Arabia's status as a swing producer declines during the next several years. Although the Persian Gulf states' share of world crude markets has dropped since the 1970s, as production levels have stagnated and other international suppliers have expanded their exports, the Gulf states' market share is likely to rise in coming years because of the region's reserve base. While there may be short-term increases over the next several years in non-Persian Gulf oil production, all major production increases from 2010–2020 are projected to come from the Gulf, with a significant percentage of those increases likely to come from Saudi Arabia.

During a period of tight global energy markets, the importance of this geopolitical and geoeconomic reality should not be underestimated. Saudi Arabia's unique reserve position gives it an unparalleled status as a swing producer. Looking well into the future, only Saudi Arabia, among the major oil producers, will have the capacity to mitigate short-term spikes in the price of oil by increasing production. Notions that other states—e.g., Russia—could assume a comparable role seem fanciful.[3]

---

3 See Fiona Hill, Shibley Telhami, et al., "Does Saudi Arabia Still Matter? Differing Perspectives on the Kingdom and its Oil," *Foreign Affairs,* November/December 2002.

These considerations underscore the importance for the Bush Administration of doing everything possible to enhance prospects for long-term stability in the kingdom. Many of the same factors that have driven a certain measure of U.S.-Saudi estrangement since the September 11 attacks have also raised doubts in the United States and other Western countries about Saudi Arabia's long-term stability. Just as renewing U.S.-Saudi strategic cooperation will require new thinking on the part of President Bush and his national security team, incorporating the goal of promoting Saudi stability into U.S. foreign policy will also require some significant mid-course corrections by the Bush Administration as it embarks on its second term in office.

STRATEGIC OPTIONS

Given the imperative of Saudi support for key U.S. policy objectives, the low probability that America and its allies can substantially reduce their dependence on hydrocarbons for energy, and the importance of preserving the kingdom's long-term stability, the United States needs a strategy for dealing with Saudi Arabia that improves the level of Saudi cooperation on important regional and energy issues while simultaneously encouraging genuine (if incremental) liberalization in the kingdom. There are four alternative, if not universally mutually exclusive, options for doing this from which a reelected Bush Administration could choose.

OPTION 1

There is, first of all, the prescription of "creative destruction": that is, to promote radical reform—effectively, regime change in the kingdom—above all else. This option presupposes that the Saudi regime is so inherently corrupt and ideologically irreconcilable to long-term U.S. interests in the region that virtually any likely alternative would be preferable, from an American perspective, to the status quo. Operationalizing this option would entail, at a minimum, a fundamental change in America's declaratory posture toward the Saudi regime, perhaps even a public determination that the kingdom is, in fact, an enemy of the United States in the context of the war on terror.

This option would seem congruent with President Bush's self-declared "forward strategy of freedom" for the region. However, it carries serious risks for U.S. interests. Given the urgency of U.S. concerns about terrorism and energy, the United States does not have the luxury of waiting for a scenario of radical transformation to play itself out. Moreover, the forces of moderation in Saudi society are sufficiently weak, relative to more conservative Islamist elements, that it is far from clear that the "destruction" of the Saudi state in the near-to-medium term would be "creative" of something more enlightened. Indeed, the most likely alternative to rule by the House of Saud is not the ascendance of liberal democrats but a seizure of power by radical Islamists hostile to the strategic and energy interests of the United States.

OPTION 2

Second, there is an argument that the United States should become more publicly demanding of the Saudis on a host of issues, such as energy, terrorist financing, educational reform, and eliminating religious extremism and intolerance. This approach should appropriately be part of any Administration's posture toward Saudi Arabia, but critical rhetoric, in isolation from other policy tools, can only go so far in defining a more productive U.S.-Saudi relationship. There are significant limits on Washington's potential negative leverage for sanctioning Saudi noncooperation; as noted above, those limits may be becoming more pronounced as China emerges as a major consumer of Persian Gulf (including Saudi) oil. In addition, America's extremely low standing with the Saudi public makes it harder for the regime to accede to public U.S. demands.

In isolation, this approach also runs a risk of emboldening those enemies of the Saudi regime who are far more inimical to U.S. interests than the status quo. Jimmy Carter has been criticized for advocating internal reform in the shah's Iran in ways that emboldened anti-Western forces while, in the end, being unprepared to support a regional ally at a time of crisis, setting the stage for the major strategic failure that led to the establishment of the Islamic Republic of Iran. President Bush will surely want to avoid a similar outcome in Saudi Arabia.

OPTION 3

Third, the United States could pursue more intensive engagement with the Saudi regime on matters of strategic importance to the United States, in a manner at least somewhat analogous to the approach that Washington has pursued since September 11, 2001 toward Pakistan, but with a larger role for discussion of internal reform issues. To some degree, the Bush Administration has adopted such a course (with limited but real success) with regard to seeking greater Saudi cooperation on counterterrorism issues such as terrorist financing. But Washington still has much work to do with Riyadh on the counterterrorism front, and the Administration has been slow to apply this approach to winning Saudi cooperation on other strategic issues, or to the encouragement of significant economic and political reform in the kingdom.

To be effective, a strategy of bilateral engagement has to go beyond exhortation and public criticism to allow for true give-and-take over both sides' strategic needs. In the Saudi context, the United States would need to be prepared for a serious conversation about how it might be willing to modify some of its regional policies (e.g., in Iraq) to accommodate Saudi interests and concerns. Moreover, the United States would need to be prepared to structure its pursuit of internal reform in the kingdom—particularly

political and social reform—in such a way as to make clear that it was not interested in encouraging reform in a manner that would fundamentally destabilize Saudi rule. Leaders and publics in the kingdom, in the region, and internationally must perceive that the fundamental motive for U.S. support to internal reform in Saudi Arabia must be to increase the chances for a continuation of the longstanding strategic partnership between Washington and Riyadh.

OPTION 4

Finally, there is a more strategically ambitious option: to leverage the potential influence of other regional allies and focus U.S. expectations of the Saudis through the establishment of a regional security framework for the Persian Gulf. While it seems misplaced to seek to extend the Organization for Security and Cooperation in Europe (OSCE) to the Middle East, the OSCE could serve as a model for constructing a regional security framework for Saudi Arabia, its neighbors, and key external players. Based on the OSCE experience, such a framework would need to be inclusive in its membership (encompassing states with which the United States has problematic relations as well as U.S. allies), comprehensive in its substantive scope (encompassing issues of economic and political transformation as well as more traditional security problems), and rooted in the principle of cooperative security through the application of mutually agreed norms (i.e., peaceful resolution of conflicts, noninterference in the internal affairs of other states, and respect for human rights).

A regional security framework for the Persian Gulf should include, at a minimum, the United States, the members of the Gulf Cooperation Council, and Iraq; to be effective, the framework would also need to include Iran. As Kenneth Pollack has noted, the prospect of membership could be an important "carrot" in our Iran policy; moreover, this prospect would reassure

Saudi Arabia and other members that the United States was serious about putting in place a meaningful post-Saddam security regime for the Gulf.

There are many reasons for the Bush Administration to support the creation of a regional security framework for the Persian Gulf. A regional security framework could be drawn out of an institutionalized "contact group" on Iraq, as described in Kenneth Pollack's essay. Such a framework is also likely to be an important element in a "grand bargain" between the United States and Iran. With regard to improving Saudi support for U.S. objectives, the logic of a regional security framework is analogous to the logic for institutionalizing regional cooperation on Iraq through a contact group or creating a security forum as part of a U.S.-Iranian grand bargain: a regional mechanism allows participants to cooperate on a sustained basis with U.S. goals without appearing to be responding directly to a U.S. diktat and while addressing their own legitimate security concerns on terms acceptable to the United States.

CRAFTING A POLICY

The most promising approach for improving Saudi cooperation with U.S. goals in the near-to-medium term while promoting gradual but genuine liberalization in the medium-to-long term is likely to be a combination of the third and fourth options described above.

The first option—"creative destruction"—would derail vital U.S. interests in the short term and almost certainly prove counterproductive to U.S interests in the longer term. Indeed, the starting point for serious policymaking regarding Saudi Arabia should be an acknowledgment by the president and his senior advisers that the House of Saud is the only alternative, for the foreseeable future, to an Arabian peninsula ruled by militant Islamists.

The second option—becoming more publicly demanding of the Saudis—may be occasionally employed, on an ad hoc basis, but, because of the limits on Washington's negative leverage with the Saudi regime, will not produce sustained results if it is the primary basis for U.S. policy.

The core of U.S. policy toward Saudi Arabia for the Bush Administration's second term should reflect an integration of the third and fourth options: more intensive bilateral engagement with the Saudi leadership combined with the establishment of security arrangements for the Gulf region. Certainly, Washington needs a more extensive and intensive bilateral dialogue with Riyadh than it presently conducts. At this point in their troubled partnership, the United States and Saudi Arabia do not talk with one another enough, and when they do talk, they increasingly talk past one another rather than with one another. This must change if the partnership is to be repaired.

The Bush Administration should build on its success so far in improving counterterrorism cooperation with the kingdom to institutionalize an ongoing and regular dialogue with the Saudis, through multiple, high-level channels, on the range of outstanding counterterrorism and regional security issues. And, the Administration must be willing to broaden the focus of its high-level dialogue with the Saudis to deal forthrightly with expectations and modalities for the encouragement of reform in the kingdom.

At the same time, the United States should anchor an expanded and intensified dialogue in a regional security framework established along the lines described above. These two tracks of a new Saudi policy should be mutually reinforcing; ideally, a more robust bilateral dialogue with the Saudis would help Washington maximize the gains from establishing a regional security framework. At the same time, the operation of the regional security framework would facilitate a more productive bilateral dialogue.

With regard to specific issues on which the United States wants greater cooperation from the Saudis, an approach combining bilateral and regional engagement would be more effective than a purely bilateral approach. For example, a regional security framework could establish regional norms and standards on issues such as counterterrorism, where smaller GCC states such as the United Arab Emirates are more forward-leaning than the kingdom. These norms could then be used to leverage improved Saudi performance in specific areas, such as terrorist financing, but without the Saudis appearing to succumb to U.S. pressure.

Properly constituted, a regional mechanism would also provide a link between America's interest in improving Saudi cooperation on regional issues with its interest in encouraging reform. When Crown Prince Abdallah first promulgated his Arab reform charter in 2003, he had no venue in which to present the idea other than the Arab League, which proved useless as a forum for implementing concrete reforms. As a result, his reform idea went nowhere, which made it even more difficult for Abdallah to implement his reform agenda at home. A regional mechanism that included various aspects of reform (economic, educational, social, etc.) in its mandate would provide cover to Abdallah and those around him interested in gradual liberalization in Saudi Arabia. Moreover, in a regional forum, the example of smaller Gulf states that are well ahead of the kingdom in reform (such as Bahrain or Qatar) could be adduced in a manner that the Saudis would not find humiliating.

A regional security framework could give the Saudis positive incentives for cooperating with various U.S. goals in the region, beyond the negative incentive of avoiding Washington's censure. The Saudis have grown increasingly uncertain about the U.S. commitment to defend the kingdom. A more systematic bilateral dialogue would address some of that uncertainty; a regional

framework backed by the United States might provide additional reassurance that the kingdom's fundamental security needs would be addressed. By recasting the traditional link between Saudi security and an American "umbrella," a regional security framework would also incentivize more constructive behavior from the Saudis on oil pricing.

A regional security framework with a relatively broad mandate could also establish badly needed "rules of the road" for regional states in a post-Saddam environment, which would be highly valued by the Saudis. Furthermore, this regional framework could also convey to the Saudi leadership that, while the United States expects better cooperation from the Saudis and wants to see significant changes in Saudi society to bring the kingdom into the globalized world of the 21st century, Washington will nonetheless work with the reform-minded elements of the royal family and Saudi establishment to achieve these goals. This could be a politically acceptable way for the Bush Administration to reassure a dubious Saudi establishment that it does not seek the implosion of the Saudi state.

If the Bush Administration were to pursue this approach to managing the U.S.-Saudi relationship, it could facilitate a much needed renewal of the sixty-year strategic partnership between the two countries. It would also encourage a process of gradual but real liberalization in the kingdom—the best course for preserving long-term stability in a country of critical importance not only to the United States, but to the international economy as a whole.

THE SABAN CENTER FOR MIDDLE EAST POLICY

The Saban Center for Middle East Policy was established on May 13th, 2002 with an inaugural address by His Majesty King Abdullah II of Jordan. The establishment of the Saban Center reflects the Brookings Institution's commitment to expand dramatically its research and analysis of Middle East policy issues at a time when the region has come to dominate the U.S. foreign policy agenda.

The Saban Center provides Washington policymakers with balanced, objective, in-depth and timely research and policy analysis from experienced and knowledgeable people who can bring fresh perspectives to bear on the critical problems of the Middle East. The center upholds the Brookings tradition of being open to a broad range of views. Its central objective is to advance understanding of developments in the Middle East through policy-relevant scholarship and debate.

The center's establishment has been made possible by a generous founding grant from Haim and Cheryl Saban of Los Angeles. Ambassador Martin S. Indyk, Senior Fellow in Foreign Policy Studies, is the Director of the Saban Center. Kenneth M. Pollack is the center's Director of Research. Joining them is a core group of Middle East experts who conduct original research and develop innovative programs to promote a better understanding of the policy choices facing American decision makers in the Middle East. They include Tamara Wittes who is a specialist on political reform in the Arab world; Shibley Telhami who holds the Sadat Chair at the University of Maryland; Shaul Bakhash an expert on Iranian politics from George Mason University; Daniel Byman from Georgetown University, a Middle East terrorism expert; and Flynt Leverett a former senior CIA analyst and Senior Director at the National Security Council who is a specialist on Syria and Lebanon. The center is located in the Foreign Policy Studies Program at Brookings, led by Vice President and Director, James B. Steinberg.

The Saban Center is undertaking original research in five areas: the implications of regime change in Iraq, including post-war nation-building and Gulf security; the dynamics of the Iranian reformation; mechanisms and requirements for fulfilling a two-state solution to the Israeli-Palestinian conflict; policy for Phase III of the war on terror, including the Syrian challenge; and political change in the Arab world.

The center also houses the ongoing Brookings Project on U.S. Policy Towards the Islamic World which is generously funded by the State of Qatar and directed by National Security Fellow Peter W. Singer. The project focuses on analyzing the problems that afflict the relationship between the United States and the Islamic world with the objective of developing effective policy responses. It includes a task force of experts, an annual dialogue between American and Muslim intellectuals, a visiting fellows program for specialists from the Islamic world, and a monograph series.